Dedication

This book is dedicated to husband Jim, children Kirsty, James and Andrea. I especially thank Andrea and other 'daughter' Angela for their technological input. Without this the book would not be born.

1

ALL MY BIG FAT SCOTTISH WEDDINGS

Art Deco Themes and 1971 Dinosaurs

Heather the bride was fully animated. "So we'll want to continue the Great Gatsby theme into the limousines, the flowers and the reception. And we'd love a champagne waterfall tower RIGHT next to the Art Deco cake. It will have to be four tiers at least 'cos I want it stacked, not tiered," she tried to sketch this with her fingers, like a kind of sign language. Then she chewed on her lip nervously and leaned into me, demonstrating how deeply serious all of this was to the success of her wedding. "You know, champagne waterfall towers are VERY Great Gatsby."

"I know. We've done a few of them before, though not always because of the deco theme." I had to smile at her enthusiasm. She was bubbling over more than any champagne waterfall.

"It would be great to get the champagne ACTUALLY WATERFALLING just before the toasts and speeches." She turned to her mesmerized groom. "Right, Malcolm?"

Malcolm nodded dutifully. Armed with his apparent reassurance, Heather moved on rapidly to the next item on her themed agenda. She pulled the invitation sample album onto her designer-jeaned knee and pointed a professionally manicured finger at the evocative Roaring Twenties style wedding invitation which clearly represented all her hopes and dreams….

"Oh! I saw this earlier. Just have a look at it!" I imagined I saw a wee trickle of happy champagne tears flow down her carefully made up cheekbones. I recognized those 'happy' tears. We had them all the time. Unhappy tears flowed occasionally, too – but happy ones were, fortunately, much more common in our establishment.

"This invitation is IT," she screamed as she turned the invite sample book around to show me. "Exactly. It kind of sums up everything I – no, I mean we – want. Doesn't it Malcolm?"

Malcolm nodded dutifully.

"I mean, it's a kind of guide for the whole style of the wedding. Like a –a- prototype, yeah?"

It was now my turn to nod dutifully. And why not, for I understood perfectly. We had coordinated many weddings with themes in recent years. The Braveheart theme had been pretty major for a while, just a year or so before and our large storeroom still overflowed with reams of colourful Scottish tartan fabric, a surplus of purple thistle and heather headdresses - and far too many Celtic tiaras.

I mulled over some of the themes – the Bohemian which I always found difficult to put together elegantly – trying not to make it look like a Hippie theme instead. There had been Tropical – fairly difficult in a location like Scotland but we managed it with the help of tropical plants, plenty of palm leaves and the occasional plastic flamingo. Only one time did we get asked for the Rustic theme. And this only transpired because the groom's parents happened to be farmers and the bride had set her sights on their very large barn. It was brand new and quite elegant, in a barn-sort-of-way. She leapt on the idea of holding the reception there, even utilizing bales of hay as guest seats after the ceilidh music started. This kilt-flying Scottish barn dance became the penultimate characteristic that defined the desired rustic theme. I suspected the theme there became more like Braveheart meets Worzel Gummidge, than anything else.

As for our current clients, a remake of the Great Gatsby movie was being filmed at this particular time in Hollywood so Heather and her agreeable groom Malcolm would be the first clients to fully immerse themselves in the trendy spirit of the Roaring Twenties. Others would follow, for sure. But Heather set great importance on being the first. They were an attractive couple. She was tall, buxom and glamourous with thick red hair cascading over her broad shoulders. Malcolm was dark, swarthy looking and equally broad-shouldered, but his mannerisms were anything but tough. Most grooms let the bride take over at these initial meetings but so far I hadn't heard a whisper of a sound of Malcolm's voice at all.

Yes, themes were very big now, I reflected silently as I noted the order.

"What do you suggest for the table flowers?" Heather went on.

I proposed narrow, vertical arrangements with some ostrich feathers and lots of pearls.

"I'll get some prepared samples to you shortly for approval. It would be best to avoid colour –

ignoring the bridesmaids completely, no matter their dress shade – it should look better in all white with either gold or silver. We'll do both for the samples."

We continued with this early stage of planning, paying attention to the detail. With themed weddings, every minutiae had to be appropriate. This was March and the big day was to be August of the following year, almost eighteen months away. I had already cleared the dates and availability, of course, so it was all good there. But a couple of other factors niggled at me, particularly the dresses.

"You want specially designed dresses for yourself and the two bridesmaids so we have to focus on all that quite soon. I'll set up appointments before you leave today." It was important that she organized her group for initial discussions on designs and measurements to get the ball rolling - so I didn't let up. "Remember, bespoke always takes time and we don't want a last minute rush at the height of the season. Plus - your date isn't that far away for planning purposes."

I looked steadfastly at her for reassurance on these points and she smiled apologetically.

"I know what you mean. I hope there's enough time, because it wasn't meant to be like this. You see we pushed the date forward almost six months because of my friend…"

This I had to hear. I leaned forward in my chair and looked inquiringly at the bride.

"You see, I was talking about my Gatsby theme to my pal Tracy and it turned out she wanted it too. For her wedding in late September. That would have been before our original date - the following April - so she would have been the first to have my dream. Imagine! I was heart-broken. Totally torn up about it. I HAD to try and get in first which meant pushing the date forward to next August." I realized for the first time just how extremely vital this theme was to our Heather.

"It's been a lot of work trying to convince our families to shove it forward, what with the budget and stuff. My Mum is gonna get another part-time evening job to help pay for it all. And Malcolm here is working double shifts at the electronic factory. That should help, too. I mean, we HAVE to get our dream wedding, no matter what, so I'm sure we'll manage. Won't we, Malcolm?"

Malcolm nodded dutifully.

I left them poring over photography sample albums and took a break. As I sipped some water in the back room I started to mull over our modern brides' notions on their elaborate weddings, their themes. In many cases, like this one - their oneupmanship goals. Sometimes it seemed that nothing was ever too good for them. If they could afford the fanfare they went for it – and I really couldn't blame them. Normality now was getting married with a huge, celebratory party after three, five, ten years or more of living together. Most times the pageboys and flowergirls were their own children following them down the aisle.

Social and sexual norms now meant there was no pressure to tie the knot. No longer was there an embarrassed, pregnant bride looking for a dress that would still fit for her wedding two or three months ahead. No, that stuff was all in the past, forty years before, back in 1971 when I launched my business idea. I glanced approvingly around my large, elegant salon at our latest detached shop premises and reflected on the thousands of weddings I had produced over that time. A much simpler time.

In auld lang syne we seemed to have no 'themes'. The majority of my customers came to me to check out hiring pretty dresses for the wedding party. Dresses that were fresh and affordable. They had been mostly open to ideas about protocol and compared to millennium brides, easily pleased. Also, I used to deal with brides who were being married for traditional, solid reasons. To be with their new husband was one. Living together was still a definite no-no back then, so if you wanted love's young dream, then you got married. I'm sure almost all of the girls I dealt with in the early seventies would have been in big trouble at home if they had hinted at the term 'living together' to Mum and Dad. It just wasn't being done. The majority of brides walked out of the family home, where they resided with their parents, to be wed.

I had set out in 1971 to create a dress hire service only, the Bridal Boutique, which drew in customers from Coatbridge itself and other surrounding towns in Lanarkshire. Subsequently, well before the millennium dawned our national advertising had moved onto specifying us as 'Scotland's Complete, Unique Wedding Specialists'. We had accumulated clients from Glasgow to Inverness, while many flew in from overseas.

In 1971 most of my customers arrived not by plane – or even by car. They travelled to me by bus and saved a few pennies for their fare home after they had given me the pound or so deposit to secure their outfits. The average bride's outfit for hire was twelve to sixteen pounds – for everything.

I had seen many changes with all of these weddings over the decades. The country began to change, life began to change and of course weddings became more ambitious, too. Naturally, they reflected the lifestyles of my clients as they chose to use posh hotels or noble castles to host their wedding receptions. But I recalled when the church hall or the Cooperative hall was almost always the venue of choice - if you were lucky. Occasionally the modest budget would demand that the reception be held at home – not in a fashionable marquee – but in the front living room.

I finished my water and mentally shelved my little nostalgia trip to rejoin Heather and Malcolm and explore their thoughts on the photography.

"Whoever you choose as photographer will be in touch with you shortly to go over the finer details personally. Based on availability, of course," I had to remind them. Basically, their date was clear for us to coordinate the wedding, but their actual choice of photographer was not guaranteed until I checked that specific individual.

Heather revealed that she had fallen in love with a particular sample album from Jerry Manning, one of our most accomplished snappers.

"It's great how he places everybody for the photos, not like most photographers. And the black and white shots are brilliant, especially when they have a wee dot of colour, like the pink roses in the bride's bouquet, or the trainbearer's dress. Fabulous!" She had obviously had another idea. I could see by her eyes that it was a biggie.

"Why don't we make ALL the photos black and white, just like back in the day. Real Gatsby, for sure! Eh, Malcolm?"

Malcolm nodded dutifully.

I had to tell her that this was not uncommon nowadays, fashionable black and white photography being considered more artistic for the creative photographer. I also added – goodness knows why - that we would not have to hark back to the 20's to find black and white pictures, in the 1970's this was still the norm.

"Really?" Heather seemed fascinated about the dark days of the 70's.

I was on a nostalgic roll. "Yes, some wedding albums did sport a few colour pictures, but the mainstay of an album would have been monotone. Black and white photos weren't considered 'artistic or fashionable then'. Most couples were just stuck with not having much choice, really...."

"Oh! Okay!" Heather had been zealously listening to my ramblings. I should have been flattered that she had paid any attention whatsoever to my history lesson.

"You said that in the 70's people mostly got black and white photos? The 70's! You know, that would be a great theme for a wedding too," she said excitedly, searching for an enthusiastic response from her spiritless groom. There was none.

I tried to stop myself from feeling uptight about her statement, but failed miserably. As someone who was married in the 1970's and created my business in the 1970's, I started to take umbrage from the suggestion that I was a relic, a period piece – a theme, even. The 70's wasn't a decade to be recognized as antique, not at all. Of course it HAD been almost forty years at that point, but the era was still there in my psyche, in my being. Perhaps even the dauntless Heather sensed my bristling with indignation. She started to back off a little.

"Well, you know… I think I REALLY still want the Great Gatsby wedding. But a 1970's theme, now that would be brilliant, too." She turned to the hapless groom.

"Wouldn't it Malcolm?"

Of course, Malcolm nodded dutifully. I was indignant.

The 70's as a wedding theme? It was absolutely ridiculous! Why, the 70's was only just yesterday! How dare she! I deruffled my old, wilted feathers, took some more booking notes and simply pretended not to hear….

In the Beginning

It certainly was a zany way to launch my future empire. I mean, who opens a bridal salon in their big spare bedroom? Spare bedrooms were synonymous with housing guests or hoarding junk but I still felt I could do it. I just hoped that my new neighbours, the Mazarolli sisters, wouldn't object.

The elderly Mazarolli sisters wanted an explanation about what was going on upstairs in our recently purchased, newly refurbished, all mod cons three bedroom Victorian flat. And they deserved an explanation. Yes, they did. However, when it came, two pairs of brown eyes almost popped out of the large sockets on their twin-like, ruddy, moon-shaped, shiny faces. I gulped nervously and tried desperately to look mature before this pair of stout little spinsters who were much more than two world wars older than me.

"Well, I've had a few groups of women coming up to visit me, yes. You obviously noticed them, yeah - well, you see - I've just started a bridal hire business at home!"

Whatever they had imagined I was about as they peeked through their yellowed white lace curtained window overlooking our shared courtyard, it was obviously – certainly - not that. Of course I should have approached them weeks before, shortly after we newlyweds had moved in. I had known then that a business would be created, so enlightening them about my plans would have been a good idea. After all, they were our only neighbours and it would have been courteous.

But also on reflection – what on earth did they think was happening at our flat? Certainly, for one or two evenings each week a number of young nubile ladies, mini-skirted and fashionable had been ascending the stairs to our shangrila. Excited, giggling and armoured against the autumn nip in fake furs and vinyl or leather coats, coupled with the ubiquitous, funky white vinyl knee high boots, they would have been a mesmerizing sight to our elderly neighbours.

From this flood of femininity the Mazarollis just might have been impressed by how popular and sociable I was – but no matter. I never did find out how their minds happened to be boggling....

"In yer hoose?" Elsa, the elder of the two was incredulous. "I know it's a decent-size flat, but still..."

"Yes," I threw back my head, exerting every ounce of confidence I could muster. "I'm using one of the spare rooms and I'm managing fine so far. No complaints." I was trying not to sound defensive, believing it would weaken my stance.

But I did want my only neighbours to react agreeably, rather than be antagonistic. So I forced a smile. "Have YOU any complaints?" I asked sweetly.

Rosa, the quieter sibling, changed her rigid stance. She was now almost apologetic and I was sure she was experiencing relief. Pushing back a few strands of charcoal grey hair from her makeup-free face and probably unaware of Elsa glaring at her, she even seemed to find a frisson of delight in the idea.

"Well, no' ree-ee-eely." I could still sense some doubt. "In fact, it's quite nice to see a bit of life for a change. I'm sure there will be no rumpus, will there? Not when it involves just women."

Suddenly the hopeful expression on her weathered face started to fade and she turned to her sister as if for moral support.

"We are talking about women only, aren't we? We've only seen women so far. There won't be any, any....MEN, or anything like that. Will there?"

I swear I detected a tiny shudder at this point.

I assured her that the appearance of any hairy-legged members of the opposite gender would be minimal indeed.

I set off up the twenty-odd well-worn steps to my home and business place and turned to try bolstering them again. I was quite earnest. Or maybe I felt guilty.

"It will be fine. I'm sure you won't be inconvenienced. Look, why don't you come upstairs for tea on Sunday and see my sct-up? You'll like it, really."

As they stood at the door of their little one storey cottage overlooking the small courtyard we shared, I finally detected a softening of attitude.

In unison they mumbled what I took to be a form of acquiescence.

"Och, that would be nice."

Elsa took charge once more.

"We both take milk and sugar and we like our tea nice and strong. Thank ye."

No Earl Grey or Darjeeling required then, I suspected. P.G. Tips would be the order of the day.

Anyhow, the dreaded deed was done. For some time I had been unsure how the women would react to my business venture, or more to the point, the lack of notification regarding its birth. I guess I should have anticipated some resentment from quiet folks who had resided here since infancy, mostly leading a sheltered and isolated life.

As a couple, we did represent an upheaval. Modernity. Change, even. The flat now owned by us had, many years before, belonged to the women's Italian immigrant parents and they had been raised in it, above the family business below, an ice-cream shop and café. Now that café was a sports shop, facing out to the busy main street beyond the entry lane to our courtyard. Since the area we all inhabited happened to be more commercial than residential, I hadn't required planning approval for my project - an encouraging factor in my decision to move forward.

Residentially speaking, there were just the Mazarollis and us, myself and my new husband of a few months. I suppose we were of great interest to them at the time, bridal business or not. We were young and fashionable professionals launching ourselves on the ocean of life. He, a zealous high-school teacher and I a keen-eyed editorial staffer with a large Glasgow based book publisher. I loved my job but I had harboured hankerings to start my own business. Having just recently experienced the dubious competence of our local wedding industry, I had opted to try retail gown hire for brides and their attendants. Why dresses? At the time, there was nothing locally for a bride who wished to rent wedding gear, making Glasgow the only option. The offerings there were not remarkable either, and I guess I thought I could do a better job.

My little upstairs dress shop ticked over nicely. Within weeks of inception the phone was ringing regularly for appointments – evenings only and Saturday mornings, at first. Certainly my full time publishing career was still paramount so I dipped my toes gradually into this new world of business. But I enjoyed the whole experience of meeting new people and assisting them with their weddings. As I look back on it now, it was quite amazing that my customers showed little surprise at my 'shop in the spare room'. I believe they felt quite comfortable being in someone's home – it was certainly a little different.

The truth was the location of the flat was great for my purposes, being right in the centre of our bustling industrial Lanarkshire town of Coatbridge, which was less than ten miles from Glasgow city. For years the creation of iron works had stamped this place. It had been pervaded with the redolence and residue of blast furnaces and the stench of smelted iron. The mélange of crossbred architecture, soiled to a filthy black and grey with the aftermath of its smokestack toil, adorned the streets. The town was a testimony to centuries of such pollution and had earned itself the dubious recognition of being foremost in the iron and steel industry of Scotland. The manufacturing had certainly brought even greater wealth to already rich industrialists but mostly a form of meagre subsistence to its workers. The lifeblood of its people still seemed to run from the smelted metal even though, by the seventies, much of the industry had wound up.

With so many churches in the area, churches of every denomination, there were always plenty of weddings going on and I was confident that I could harness some of that business. I advertised every week in the columns of our local newspaper, proudly flaunting my brand new telephone number, guardedly presented to me at last by the General Post Office which was responsible at that time for the supply of phone lines – and the actual phones themselves. The average GPO waiting time to get set up was about six months but we had wisely applied very early before our actual wedding and the final closing date of our house purchase.

So now one of our two large, spare bedrooms was furnished with three antique, duck-egg blue painted armoires to house my growing collection of exclusively white wedding gowns and a big rainbow of bridesmaid dresses. I had acquired a handsome full length mirror which worked efficiently at the time and still did so almost forty years later in a posher situation as it reached it's sixth and final business location. Fortunately at that time we as a couple never experienced any major inconvenience or feelings of being cramped due to the business. The flat was spacious. Every room was generous and square, high ceilinged and adorned with regal crown molding throughout. The long, wide hallway had an ornate ceiling which boasted a very grand rose plaster medallion and was further embellished with a British Home Stores crystal chandelier which I fancied looked elegant to receive my very important clients. A high quality thick, deep gold, plain fitted carpet framed the scene.

Hard Rock Café had just been born. Innovatively I was all set, too. It was 1971 and I had a new husband, a new home and a new business – complete with a new ivory coloured telephone. This stood on the demi-lune table in our wedgewood blue with brilliant white trim painted hallway, of course. The hall was where all respectable phones belonged at that time.

The flat had the equivocal advantage of being a few metres away from a busy bus stop. This had links to a main local and city bus route which my customers could access in order to reach me. In the early seventies not everyone owned motor cars so public transport was in great demand. Business wise, the bus stop was definitely a plus factor. However, there were domestic drawbacks. Hordes of people, a few of them definitely undesirable, would hang around the bus stop at the little lane leading to the flat, unwittingly - and often wittingly - blocking the way. Due to the profusion of pubs in the town centre, many of these folks were displaying the effects of several small sherries…..

There was, and still is, a tendency for any drunks in this area of Lanarkshire to refer to every male as 'Jimmy'. Perhaps this is the case because half of the local male population seems to use this signature. Anyhow, still blessed with another spare bedroom, in spite of using one for business, we often housed visiting friends. One amigo came to see us, all the way from the USA. Of course he couldn't have been named Brad or Chuck like every other self respecting American. No. He had the misfortune to be called James and was understandably confused on the occasions he entered the lane to our home and was effusively and personally addressed by the local inebriates.

"How come they know my name?"

He would ask this, naïve, agape and wide-eyed, as he was bombarded with cordial, local vernacular greetings.

"Hullaw'rerr Jimmy!"

"Are ye' alright, Jimmy?"

"Enjoy yer night, Jimmy."

"See you, Jimmy, ye're a right stoater…."

We tried to explain but this seemed to cause more confusion. Just enjoy, was our advice and be happy not to have received the 'Glasgow Kiss'. Oh, dear! More explanation required…….

Being central, my clients found me easily, even if the entryway to our courtyard from the main street was a trifle dark for evening appointment guests. Attached to the lane and courtyard's exterior gable wall was the only source of light. It was a large coach-style lamp originating from the Victorian era and although it was cute, was rendered hopeless by its small, weak, barely flickering gas flame. Yes….gas.

Accepting that I was the new kid on the block I opted to politely defer to the Mazarolli sisters whom I had no problem locating, since they seemed to spend most of their surplus recreational time spying on me through their little window. They had seen me staring up quizzically at the offending gaslight and duly opened their faded pea green door to proffer assistance. I nodded to them in greeting then pointed upwards.

"Does the leerie come by every night to light this?"

I was, as I thought, joking as I reflected on Robert Louis Stevenson's delightful childhood poem, The Lamplighter. Apparently not so.

"Leerie? No. Not for a couple o' years now," Elsa explained intently, obviously racking her brain to recall leerie's last visit. Suddenly her expression changed to one of almost prissy pride. "But, ye' know, this is the new kind o' flame that jist stays on a' the time. Ye dinna' need a leerie to light it every night. "

She made it sound like a promotional summation of the latest computer technology. In spite of this, I had another idea.

"Perhaps I'll phone the local authorities and find out if an electric light could be installed instead. The gas flame is far too weak."

As if to convince myself and my neighbours about the gravity of the situation, I rolled my eyes up again towards the pathetic flame, holding dearly onto life within its old glass shelter.

"Would that be alright with you both?"

It was remiss of me to presume sympathy for my cutting edge ambitions.

"It'll no' make much difference tae us," said Rosa, shrugging and glancing as usual towards Elsa for sisterly approval.

"But ah'm no sure ye'll get an electric one. The cooncil are that slow and they hate spending money…"

Elsa concurred.

"Electric light! Naw, they'll no spend tuppence. And the best o' it is, if ye think this isnae' such a good flame, then that's the burgh's fault. They were the wans that changed it."

Rosa jumped in with the clincher.

"Aye. It wis workin' fine till they converted it tae North Sea gas last year."

So much for progress. I reeled from this knock-out punch.

"North Sea…." I was almost speechless. "You mean they actually did a gas conversion when they could have just set the place up with proper, modern lighting? Unbelievable."

I should not have been so shocked. At that time Scotland was rejoicing in it's oil-rich status as precious oil and gas was being pumped out profusely from the bountiful North Sea between north-east Scotland and south-west Norway. Plainly there was so much to go around, the powers-that-be had initiated The Great Gas Conversion Caper – even converting seriously aged coach lamps. I should have known. In our area, local residents didn't nickname the local authorities 'Clown Touncil' for nothing.

I shook my head disbelievingly as I climbed the steps to the flat, foolishly assuming that we had wound up our informative chat. I was halfway there when Elsa cleared her throat, making it clear that she was still on a mission to educate me further. She had obviously been racking her brain.

"Now wait a wee minute. Jist wait till ah think." She fussily tugged and tidied her rather tight and worn wrap-around apron, her uniform. It was definitely not a fashion statement but like her sister, she seemed to wear a fresh, colour-faded one every day. Today's was a washed-out burgundy and blue Paisley pattern.

She had requested a wee minute but I wasn't sure that I had that much time to spare. For as I looked up to the dusky heavens I foresaw a sinister charcoal cloud about to burst upon us. Happily, Elsa's much anticipated thought came forthwith.

"Now. Dae ye' mind, Rosa? That bloke who came here last September tae see aboot the lamp? Ye know, it wisnae' a leerie that came to convert it. Naw, naw, it wis somebody else. B'jings, whit title did they give him again….?"

27

Suddenly she smiled victoriously, if semi-toothlessly, as the thought finally struck ground zero.

"He wis a…a…yes! He wis a 'PUBLIC LIGHTING AND MAINTENANCE INSPECTOR'. There!"

She clearly considered this title to be of singularly regal status.

"Aye, that's it. A PUBLIC LIGHT……"

She was undoubtedly on a roll and would have to be restrained. So I did.

"I see. I'll get in touch with the appropriate people tomorrow. Good night, ladies!" I started to head up the stairs again to my refuge.

But there was more. Suddenly Elsa was a gushing, illuminating, fountain of knowledge.

"Ye could ask for him when you phone. He wis very nice. Because ah can even remember his name! Aye! Ye' know…. people love it when you can remember their names."

I feigned keen interest as she continued. And it WAS very interesting. But not a surprise.

"It's important that you ask for 'Jimmy'. Now, remember. 'Jimmy'. Ok?"

"Yes! Jimmy! Ok!" I yelled down the stairs.

I opened my flat door, trying not to giggle. So Jimmy was his name? I didn't have to write it down. I wondered how I could possibly forget.

The Wedding Apprentice

The Bridal Boutique was launched and ticking along nicely as I focused on filling my nice painted wardrobes with pretty dresses and accessories.

At first, sourcing gowns was done in a rather unorthodox way....I got myself lots of retail therapy. Since my stock requirements were so modest in these early days, I knew I was not yet ready to order from large wholesale suppliers who all demanded fairly sizeable minimum orders. I was still very small potatoes and opted to limit myself at first by buying wisely from bridal shops in the city.

My Glasgow office lunch breaks were regularly spent browsing around the city's wedding dress salons and scouring the clearance sale rails. For this first year of business I would reinvest every penny I received back into new gowns of all styles and sizes. I soon discovered that size variety was all important and set out to acquire at least a half dozen or so wedding gowns in every size from a ten to an eighteen. This cautious approach allowed me to build up a respectable variety of both wedding and bridesmaid dresses without an immediate large financial investment but it was a slow approach and involved several months of shopping to realise my goals. Bridal stock was expensive - so even in the sale section, the dresses I accumulated represented many hundreds of pounds.

Thankfully, most of my customers were practical, no nonsense working class girls who strived to make happy choices from my collection. They were determined to hire, not buy, for several reasons. The main one was cost. A wedding outfit at that time averaged around sixty pounds to purchase, including headgear, veil and alterations. Bearing in mind a decent salary was about seventy pounds a month, then it made sense to rent a gown. I could put out a full wedding outfit with all the accessories and including alterations, for approximately a quarter of that money – about fifteen pounds – which made hiring an attractive option. Possibly another factor which drew certain clients to me was the imbalance in wages between men and women at that time, which seems outrageous to us now, I know. Even with the Equal Pay Act of 1970 women, who were exclusively my customers, earned an average fifteen per cent less than their male cohorts on the same job. Since I only dealt with female clients at this time, it was their hard-earned pennies which appeared to pay for the wares.

But there were other reasons for hiring gowns besides cost. In those black and white days almost all of my girls discussed their post wedding housing arrangements with me. That's what women do, we air everything. A little stress relief. Anyhow, I learned that the majority of newlyweds would probably be moving in with a parent or grandparent while they put some pennies together for a house deposit or waited to ascend the council house list. Naturally, this meant a dearth of their personal space where there was definitely no room for big, puffy, redundant dresses, so purchasing was an uncomfortable prospect for many. Bridesmaids were expected to follow suit with the bride who, if she was hiring her own gown, was certainly intending to hire her attendants' outfits. However, even if a bride did decide to buy, she would often opt to simply rent the girls' dresses so I made sure I had lots of colourful maids' gowns in lots of sizes.

I enjoyed my forays to the bridal stores to stretch my supplies. One bridal centre near Sauchiehall Street in Glasgow often benefitted from my regular purchases. Since this amounted to at most, one or two dresses a fortnight – and always from the sale rail – the total spent was never elaborate. But on reflection, how many repeat customers did a bridal shop have? Well, they could have had Elizabeth Taylor, the famous actress, as a client. Miss Taylor was at that time zipping her way through a multitude of husbands. The rest of us, however, generally tripped down the aisle just once, the divorce rate still moderate in spite of the recent 1969 Divorce Reform Act making breakups easier.

Later on in my wedding career, couples would joke to me, as a compliment, "You know, we've decided that you can do ALL our weddings from now on!" But in 1971 one particular young trainee bridal assistant in a Glasgow salon began to believe she really WAS doing all MY weddings…..

"Oh, hello again, how are you? My, this is a gorgeous dress," as she wrapped it in white tissue and placed it tenderly in a posh bag. There was a little shy, slightly furtive look from under her fluttering false eyelashes. "And don't you just love the long sleeves? The seed pearls make a great feature around the neckline, don't they? You know, I wished I had seen you try it on!" Of course, I had not.

The babble continued as she looked up at me interestedly. "So I noticed you in here not so long ago buying another wedding dress." There was a slightly confused look at this stage since I remained very quiet and just smiled. "Oh, well. This one doesn't have a train so you can always use it afterwards for parties. Do you go to many parties....or weddings?"

I had no intention of spilling the beans on my new venture. Truthfully, I naively believed that if they knew I was buying for business, I could possibly be banned from the shop. Of course after several months of such subterfuge, the cheery salesgirl came to her own conclusions on the matter.

"Oh, yes. What a stunning dress. Some lucky bride is going to look lovely in this, eh?" Wink, wink.

The reactions were the same at the other retail salons I frequented. Of course I was met with side glances and strange looks, but that was all. Nothing was asked and nothing was given. I was good for their business and I guess they had to appreciate that a sale was a sale.

My own units of sale were increasing, too. Customers had begun to ask about auxiliary services, particularly flowers. I still did not want to throw myself in at the business deep end due to my full time editorial job, but I knew I could handle flower orders if I was simply an order agent. I reckoned that if I could tie up with a reliable florist who would take full responsibility and deliver the arrangements, then great. I found a local florist shop which worked well in the beginning, but the owner started to back off as his own pre-summer diary filled up, making excuses not to take my business and simply focus on his own. Realizing by this time that flowers were fairly lucrative, I sought other alternatives to keep my brides happy and continue to nurture a healthy floral area of business. But I had to have reliability. Wounded by the florist's rejection, I felt that the only one I could rely on was myself. Delegation was a skill I had to learn slowly and painfully over the years. Often I was reluctant to trust new, untried, outside sources. In the future when I had to work with myriads of people in the wedding business, it became easier. But this came with learning and experiencing just WHO to trust. At that moment I decided - publishing job or not - I would fit in some floristry classes.

This was easier said than done. I enquired at our local college but since it was already almost spring, it was too late to enroll. I was determined to find help and it came in the form of a flower arranging church group. I could join immediately and went for it – every Tuesday at 7 o'clock in Bank Memorial Church Hall. I was told to bring along some basic florist's tools and accessories, but they never mentioned the uniform. Twinsets and pearls. Almost everyone was wearing them because almost everyone there was female, grey-haired and retired. The one exception was Jeffrey, a quiet middle-aged widower whose obviously appalling lack of social life had compelled him to join in order to get out of the house.

"Well, isn't it nice to see a young 'un here!" was the chorus. And they really were the chorus. As the church choir troupe, they practised their harmonies as they pottered with the flowers, regularly breaking into 'Guide Me O Thou Great Redeemer' or 'Jerusalem' at the drop of an antique silver hatpin. Nevertheless I was overjoyed at the prospect of learning the craft of flower arranging amongst all these friendly, musical busy bees.

A tall, sturdy, very senior lady who bore the incongruous name of Reinhild Macdonald was in charge of the group and immediately let this be known to me. She had the presence and manner of a strict headmistress, from her severely permed, silver-haired coiffure right down to the elaborate spectacles and tweed skirt. She impressed me as someone who would definitely make you sit on the 'naughty' chair if you pushed her too far. Reinhild had very firm ideas about the class training process, which I began to realise might be a tad slow for my taste. It was like learning to drive in first gear. And for someone who was young and cool and possessed a tolerance level even shorter than her micro-mini leather skirt, I was on tenterhooks most of the time. Reinhild was quite unsympathetic to my ants-in-pants disposition, so she would reprimand me whenever I had the affrontery to try and speed things up.

"You haff to valk before running," she yelled. No, SCREAMED, was more like it. I mused that an extra curricular pastime for her would have been assisting the local coalman with his deliveries and yelling "Cooooaaaalll!" at the top of her multi-decibel voice. But perhaps the loudness was more forced than I had at first thought, since the bulk of the mainly over-sixties class just might have been disadvantaged by hearing impairment. I truly believed she operated on the premise that if you did not understand her lingo, you could at least hear her - for even she must have realized that her command of the Queen's English was severely lacking.

It was amazing that after twenty-five years of living in Britain, she still spoke barely pigeon English and mixed it imaginatively with her own native tongue. Her deceased husband had been a local, so I found it hard to fathom why she struggled so much with the language. When he was alive, they must have spoken to each other.... occasionally.

Reinhild's naïve confusion with the sound and arrangement of English words was achingly funny for me. While my sense of humour has certainly not diminished over the years, maturity has enabled me to suppress inappropriate mirth, but at that time I often found it impossible to contain. For me the strange thing was that as I glanced around the group looking for giggle support, invariably there was none, the class seeming to accept her eccentricities resolutely. Probably because of the generational gap, I seemed to be alone in viewing our instructor's idiosyncrasies with hilarious delight. This truly puzzled me, for the incidents were often shriekingly funny.

One example came on the run up to Easter when Reinhild, whose heart was well placed, appealed to our group to contribute chocolate eggs to a church effort. These were intended for distribution amongst underprivileged children.

"I vill be here next week, of course." She pointed to the back hall kitchen. "But eef you are comink another time, chust go to ze kitchen and lay your eggs on the big table……"

She would always cough energetically before attempting any kind of general speech so we were forewarned to pay careful attention.

"Vee are having an important fund raiser for the church in just two veeks, a jumble sale of used clothing in the church hall."

Reinhild was in charge of the event and appealed for item donations, then followed this up with an irresistible invitation to preview what was on offer.

"The committee ladies and myself are casting off ALL our clothes on Friday morning – so you must all kom then for a private and very special viewing, ya?"

As usual I glanced around to check the response, but of course everyone was totally deadpan - except Jeffrey. Just then I was sure I detected a few nervous blinks and a flush of colour on his normally blanched cheeks. Yes, he was a fan. I speculated that he must have found Reinhild's accent to be a thing of exotic beauty and perhaps it was….in comparison to the local Lanarkshire brogue.

She obviously exclusively thought in German.

"Eins, zwei, drei, vier," she mumbled as she counted out the roses which would be distributed amongst us. Again, as I studied Jeffrey's earnest face, I could see that he was quite in awe of her. Yes, he had the hots for The Widow Reinhild and I wondered if his deceased wife had been a strong, imposing character too. Jeffrey's stature was frail compared to the object of his desire. He was of respectable medium build with a hairline that had not receded totally so one could still detect wisps of a reddish gold mane now gone grey.

"Reinhild is a marvellous flower arranger, don't you think so?" He whispered this to me earnestly in the huge kitchen as we were having our ubiquitous tea and biscuits. We all nibbled on Kit Kats while Reinhild enjoyed her home made strudel. I rolled my eyes cynically. The teabreak was another irritation for me since it meant downing tools and slowing the learning process even more - for almost fifteen minutes. I should have lightened up a little, but I was so keen to learn it all quickly. I split my Kit Kat and dunked one chocolate wafer finger into my tea-filled English bone china cup nestling in its English bone china saucer. No cheap, thick mugs at this parish hall.

"Yes, she is," I had to agree. "But I feel we could move along a wee bit more speedily, you know?"

Jeffrey looked horrified. "That would mean the classes would finish quicker. Gosh, there would be nothing else for me to do on a Tuesday night."

His face took on a wistful, dreamy expression. "I dread when this all ends…"

It sounded like a great closing line to a 1950's Hollywood movie. I had to jolt myself back to reality – yes, this was simply Tuesday night in the church hall flower arranging class. But Jeffrey was right - it was supposed to be a recreational class for everyone - except me, who wanted to race through all the steps for business purposes. I found it tough to be patient and soak up Reinhild's knowledge in such a slow fashion. The progress was as slow as the spread of thick homemade jam on our occasional teatime scones. No, I wanted to drink the knowledge down fast, so fast as to make me burp. So I gulped my cooling tea down quickly, belched discreetly and skulked over to Reinhild's table. She watched me warily as I approached, both hands tensely stuffed into the tiny pockets of my little skirt. It was all reminiscent of a western movie gunfight where Reinhild was the good Sheriff and I was the baddie who had to get out of town….fast.

"I really need to know what I'm doing by the end of this month, Reinhild." It was March. "I want to start taking orders for wedding flowers then - but I have to feel more knowledgeable and confident so that I can move ahead. Do you have any textbooks you could lend me so that I can speed things up…."

The response was deafening. For a moment I feared that the glass lens in the gold-rimmed spectacles dangling from a chain around her neck would shatter. She lifted a plump, frankfurter-shaped finger to push back a stray lock of salt and pepper hair - hair that had had the audacity to trespass onto her perspiring, frowning, verboten brow.

"By the end of thees month! Vot nonsense! You are still kindergarten here! It will not kill you to wait longer. Remember thees is not killing you but is making you big and strong, ya…"

I believed she was quoting Nietzche in a totally bizarre way. But I didn't hang around long enough to figure it out and simply crawled away meekly as she roared a command to the whole assembly.

"Efferyone ees time to go back to our vork!" Then directly to my retreating figure: "Go get the wasser and I vill show you how to use oasis goot, not bad as you haff been doing here…"

That was it. I decided to relax my way through the rest of the course which, slow or not, proved to be extremely beneficial for the future of my business. I had learned how to choose appropriate blooms and suitable foliage for particular arrangements – how to prepare flowers and take care of them before the creative effort. It was indeed an artistic outlet and came with some distinction. Reinhild, at our weekly recognition segments, would even offer crumbs of praise. My offerings became regular features of the "Three Best Efforts" facet of the evenings which built my confidence no end. At last the final evening arrived when we would receive our little certificates of completion attached to our examination offering of skill and learning. Reinhild was, for once, uncharacteristically kind to everyone. This was justified for we had all produced a decent standard of arrangement. She looked very closely and slowly at my large centrepiece, checking the placement, choice of foliage. Everything. I dared to hope she would give me a good review on my certificate although it was hardly important for my purposes. She finally bellowed her approval.

"Ya, thees ees goot example of solid vork. Eet ees pretty, musst be pretty, but ees also tough and strong. No goot if eet goes kaput ok? So Miss Order Book has learned vell." She turned to me with a hint of a smile. "Remember we have to eat a peck of dirt every day before we die! Thees I have told you many times…."

Yes, she did tell me many times. But to this day I have no idea what she meant.

I gazed at her now more respectfully, making contact with her pale blue eyes, which were framed under the forbidding shelter of two very thick, bushy and unruly eyebrows. I shuffled my feet and backed up a little, anticipating perhaps a more critical, lusty assault on my shell likes.

I must have truly mastered the course. Because for once, there was none.

A Rose by Any Other Name

My business was expanding and so was I. A couple of years into my marriage I became pregnant, which prompted many changes.The main adjustment was reclaiming our flat for family living and endeavouring to relocate the Bridal Boutique elsewhere. I would now be retiring from my full time job in the city as an editorial assistant and focusing on the new baby while keeping my little business ticking over.

A few weeks before the baby was born I wobbled down to the town centre to view a vacant, single windowed shop which fitted my criteria. It was sizeable and already had fitted dress rails due to its previous existence as a ladies' dress shop. I would give it a go and work hard to achieve results, at last bringing in wholesale suppliers to stock me for wedding and bridesmaid dress sales, as well as hires. I reviewed their catalogues, and had helpful sales reps come to me at the shop, vowing that trade fairs were still not going to be part of my new curriculum. My maternal responsibilities and geographical location limited me from attending those, most of which were hundreds of miles away down south. I was laboriously busy just trying to organize the structure of new family and my new shop.

It was gratifying to achieve success with the new leg of business – flowers. The order books were looking good and I enjoyed the creative challenge this set me. Thanks to Reinhild, my skills with church and table arrangements were quite commendable but ironically, when the class wound up I was still not confident about making up bouquets and posies. This they had not covered in class, unfortunately. I set out to home school myself by taking apart some old samples of silk posies and rearranging them my own way. A lot of it was technical stuff – wiring and taping, using fresh and plastic oasis – and learning about the feathers. Ah, the feathers…..

Feather framed arrangements were fashionable at the time so I practised those, too. Since this was all extra curricular HOMEwork, the home vacuum cleaner was being worked overtime on my very plumaged living room carpet to stop the room itself looking like a chicken coop. Mainly the feathers were used with silk bouquets, and would be wired individually, then placed around the bouquet forming a corona. I would joke with brides that the feathered bouquets were practical choices – that they could always be used as dusters around the house after the big day.

During my salad days of floristry my learning curve embraced not only technical skills, but a degree of strategy – and trust. The Kinghorn wedding was one that highlighted to me again the importance of trust, of reliability. I was selfishly relieved afterwards that the lesson I had learned involved a good looking clergyman and a good natured family....

The whole Kinghorn party was delightful to deal with which was a real bonus for me since I always spent a lot of time with clients as a run up to a wedding. Doing extra services like flowers as well as dresses, meant relationships with clients became even more important and it was easy to bond with this crew for they were all positive and cheerful. All the dresses were being hired from me so there were plenty of opportunities at appointments to chat and chuckle before Moira's wedding in St. Jude's. Mum Carol was a delight, her two sisters were cheery bridesmaids and to boot, her brother Kenny was best man since she was marrying his closest friend. A family affair, right enough.

The Friday evening before the wedding I set off to deliver the church flowers, leaving the next morning free for me to make up the girls posies and deliver them late morning to the bride's home. On that nippy November evening the gothic style parish house oak double doors creaked open after I had parked on the gravel driveway. This older, slightly forbidding style of church seemed to be at odds with the fresh-faced young priest who had opened those doors - the impossibly handsome Father Monaghan. I soon found out why his large dark eyes had expressed shock and disbelief when I revealed who I was.

"Oh, no! The Kinghorns never told you then?" He ran his fingers exasperatedly through his mane of copper, curly hair and sighed loudly. "There's a funeral tomorrow morning so these flowers can't be placed till afterwards. The bereaved family made it clear about that. Can you come back in the morning, then? Plenty of time before the wedding – the funeral will be over by eleven o'clock."

Before I had time to answer he cut in again. "No! No! You know - that's absolute nonsense asking you to trek back here again. It's only two pedestals, right? One on each side of the altar? I've done enough weddings to know the layout of these things. Leave them with me and I'll get them into their positions after the funeral, ok?"

I nodded slowly, still conjugating all this unexpected news. I was uncertain about my shedding of responsibility, which I thought to be a bit unprofessional. On the other hand the layout was simple – just two pedestals – and overlooked by a priest who was clearly savvy enough to do the necessary.

Aided by Father Monaghan I took the flowers out of my estate car and placed them inside the little scullery adjacent to the kitchen. It was cool, if not cold, so I threw a couple of glasses more water into the bottom of the flowers to make sure they were well hydrated. The pale lilac ribbon attached to each container wound its way softly along the tiled floor and I thought as I left how great the arrangements looked. There were lilies and chrysanths, roses and white gypsophila galore. Thanks to Reinhild and her draconian, but effective teachings I was finally confident about the flower jobs and was really taking great artistic satisfaction from them. Yes, the Kinghorns would be chuffed with the look of the church. As I left I took a final sniff of the heady perfume, especially from the lilies. It was almost therapeutic.

I had the same proud feeling next day when I took the bouquets over to the girls. There were gasps of delight when they saw the fresh roses and gyp I had put together. Busy as they were preparing hair and makeup, everyone stopped to make a fuss over the flowers. Carol was particularly generous in her praise and as a relative newcomer to the floral art, I took great pleasure from this. I adored doing such deliveries at that time and even decades later when I would drop off bouquets I had a hand in, or flowers created by another team member, I always revelled in the joy of that moment. It was all good at the Kinghorns and I left the house feeling contented with a good job well done.....

Monday was return time for the weekend hires so I chatted away to Carol as we unwrapped the bridesmaid dresses.

"Everything go ok?" I inquired, as I retrieved the dresses and accessories from their bags before refunding the hire deposits. I was eager to know how great it all was and yes - the response was happy and positive. Maybe too happy, if that's possible. For Carol started laughing uncontrollably.

Well, I was extremely glad she wasn't crying, but what the…

"I'm sorry. Everything else was terrific. But the church flowers, ha, ha, ha," and off she went again into convulsions of laughter.

I could tell she was trying to keep a straight face. "I'm sorry, but the church flowers were a disaster." More helpless mirth ensued. In between the convulsions she spilled the story.

"You know how our son Kenny was best man to the groom and…" Chokes followed sobs of laughter again. "Well. He has a flatulence problem. Ever since he was a wee boy, in fact." The nose was being blown to bits into her hanky but still she laughed, and laughed. "The whole family is always kidding him about it."

It was difficult to catch everything amongst the muffled laughter but it slowly came tumbling out that emanating from the area of the altar during the ceremony was a horrific, pungent smell. Of course this was to assail onto the nostrils of those guests unfortunate enough to be in the front few rows, namely the extended Kinghorn clan. Carol, her husband and other relations were convinced that Kenny had been releasing suppressed wind - right there in the middle of the wedding vows.

"His Dad and I were drawing daggers at him and as he was standing side on, he could see our black looks. He just kept turning round to us grinning and shrugging his shoulders in innocence. I could have murdered him. But poor Kenny, it wasn't him at all. Ha, ha, ha! The awful smell had nothing to do with him." She started choking again.

"It was coming from the flowers." She paused for a moment to draw breath from her guffaws. "They looked fine, mind you. But Father Monaghan told us afterwards that the smell was coming from the church flowers, right enough."

What? My beautiful fresh blooms? Impossible. I immediately phoned Father Monaghan for his take on the affair.

"I feel so bad about this, it was totally my own fault what happened," he told me.

Unlike Carol, he could see nothing funny about the scenario. "After you left on Friday I decided to put the flowers outside the back door where it was cold. I thought the wee scullery wasn't cool enough, you know? Well, that was my mistake."

He did not, however, reckon on a heavy frost that November evening. "The poor flowers were affected and I never noticed. They must have frozen slightly but to be honest they looked fine and even in the church they still seemed okay, till they eventually thawed. But the smell!"

It was a relief the family saw the funny side of this little disaster and didn't blame me in the slightest. Nor were they angry with poor Father Monaghan.

"These things happen," Carol assured me with a very bright twinkle in her eye. "We forgot to tell you about the funeral and the priest made a wrong decision. So it isn't really your fault in any way…"

I didn't agree. I refunded her for the flowers because I felt this was ultimately my responsibility. I could have, and should have, returned on the morning of the wedding, but I took the simplest way out. It was part of my growing experience and outlined how easily things can go wrong, especially when you walk away from being in charge, as I did. As a wedding planner-to-be I would learn that it's good to be a control freak. Even then we can plan and organize but fate just might step in with a big, clumsy footprint.

It certainly sounded like the kind of stuff Reinhild would have said. But no – it was Robert Burns who penned this wise line.

'The best laid schemes o' mice an' men gang aft a-gley.' Absolutely.

The Chameleon

The pretty dark-haired doctor could not look me in the eye. She was too busy staring fixatedly at my large bump. "Let me check this again. You THINK you're pregnant, is that right?"

She started to fumble around agitatedly with my medical file. Oh, I was on file alright and practically on first name terms with most of the staff in our local, pre-natal clinic. Since this was my third pregnancy I anticipated being upgraded to their 'best customers' file. Or possibly their 'worst customers' file. That all depended on where you stood. Personally, I felt that I had been standing right there on that hard, tiled clinical floor for far too long, inviting the prospect of varicose veins. All of this flitted through my brain as I tried not to think about my irresponsibility, but the doctor wasn't going to let up. She looked at the chart again before glaring at me angrily.

"And this is your first visit here? Unbelievable!"

Even the kind little blonde nurse who normally held your hand sympathetically and supportively as you were being examined, was not HER usual understanding self, either. "You should have been in here months ago!" And she rolled her eyes at the doctor whilst I stood there wishing they would hurry and decide my fate or possibly allow me to run off to the ladies' room. The pressure on my bladder was excruciating.

I knew they were spot on about not getting to the clinic way earlier but honestly, there just didn't seem to be enough hours in the day at that time. Between helping my new assistant Maureen keep everything squared up in the shop, taking fresh business and producing the goods, I was always occupied. Not to mention coping with my two toddlers of three years and sixteen months, who were at home right then with my mother so that finally I could get to the doctor. On a positive note, the procrastination also came from the fact that I felt splendid, in spite of the high level of activity around me. I had been top notch with my previous pregnancies and was the same with this one. I guess I had thought that this bunny rabbit knew it all.

Nevertheless my disingenuous stance was not working with these two savvy ladies. I still didn't get to lie, or even sit down. The tall, elegant doctor spoke over the top of my head as if I was not actually there. "Ok. Let's give her a scan straightaway and try to figure out the ETA of this one."

A scan! I had never had one of these before. At that time in the late seventies scans were only given to pregnant women in exceptional circumstances, not as a routine. No, not like today when young mums seem to have their unborn babies photographed more than Kim Kardashian.

Blessedly, everything was fine and a few months later I produced a gorgeous, black-haired, text-book baby girl. But it had been a shock finding out about this third baby. Pregnant again? For the life of me, I had no idea what was causing it. The contaminated water in the old lead pipes, perhaps?

We had also just bought a new home, which had been both a joy and a nuisance, since I was also super preoccupied with having to shop for new curtains, carpets and the rest with two and a half babies in tow. Realistically, it had been a relief to get out of our flat and buy a lovely big detached home in a plush part of town. Now I had only two little steps to climb to my front door instead of the twenty-two at the flat which I had fondly named Ben Nevis. Believe me - to a very pregnant woman with two toddlers in tow and a large royalty sized pram, those stairs had been a challenge.

I finally terminated the lease on the town centre shop due to all of these intimidating factors, finally gave up my professional ambitions and finally decided to content myself for a time with motherhood. A few weeks before the new baby arrived all my stock was shipped down to our new home, boxed and carefully placed in the extremely useful and spacious attic. Bye, bye bridal business, I thought sadly. I had thousands of pounds of lovely dresses and accessories now doing nothing and it certainly bothered me that if I excavated the boxes out of there in a couple of years or so they would be either decayed or terribly out of fashion. Nevertheless, I was forced to resign myself to throwing in the nuptial towel for a couple of years…but fate had other ideas.

I wasn't long out of hospital with our latest arrival when people started to arrive at the front door, slightly jarring my domestic bliss. I was not sure what to tell them. There I was feeding baby, making soup, doing washing whilst singing 'The

Wheels on the Bus' for the sixth hundredth time and they were asking me about wedding stuff. I often wondered why, on peeking round my outside door to witness the chaos of the domestic paradise inside, they did not decide to forgo their romantic wedding plans entirely - right there and then. I became expert at keeping one eye on the friendly doorstep intruders and another on the anarchy inside.

"Yes, that's right. I had the shop up in Main Street…excuse me. PUT THAT CRAYON DOWN! NO YOU MUST NOT WRITE ON THE BABY'S FACE WITH IT. Sorry about that…..yes I had to stop for personal reasons… excuse me again…OK! MUMMY WILL TAKE YOU TO THE POTTY IN A MINUTE….. Oh, I think it's too late for the potty…..leave your phone number and I'll call you later. Is that ok? Must go just now!"

It was definitely flattering that my business had not been forgotten and I was pleased that they were seeking me out. The truth was there were customers who needed me and even with all my fresh household responsibilities, I needed them, too. I missed the adult, female company and the Bus Song was wearing a bit thin, after all. We were lucky to have a huge front lounge which we never used, preferring the big back sitting room near the kitchen – or to be more exact, near the kettle and teabags. So the attic was raided, dress rails set up in the lounge and I was off again. The Wedding Lady was relaunched. I eliminated the flowers and dress sales, focusing on hire only again – and to mostly evening appointments due to the lack of daytime child help. My business was moving back to home just like the beginning once again. At night Other Half was home from his college lecturing job and my mother had usually finished her golf games.

Fortunately, there was enough room in my strange new salon to use two huge screens as room dividers and split the area, allowing me to attend to two separate groups simultaneously. I certainly couldn't have been accused of lacking effort or ambition by taking on two parties, but I had limited evening help, had to get on with it, so juggling became second nature. And I was a woman. That's what we do. The screens offered a roomy and totally private space for each party but what was not so private was a lack of sound barrier. Everyone was privy to the hub of conversation with each group as I dashed from one side of the screen to the other assisting the girls with the goodies.

I recall one evening when I was dealing with two groups like this – each one representing a different socio-economic demographic. I hate to use the snotty word 'class' but I guess I had both working class and uppity middle class going on at the same time. Is it good to be a chameleon? I do think it's important in business and also in life, striving to blend in with our fellow human beings. Therefore I blended.

The first of my two sets of customers arrived. Denise and her well dressed, elegant mother laid down their expensive coats carefully on my elegant bergere chair as we broke ice.

"Hello, nice to meet you, Denise. You must tell me all about your wedding plans and the type of gown you're looking for. It is important, after all, for me to gauge your expectations, blah, blah, blah. I made it sound more like Bond Street rather than a room in the house.

Denise immediately felt comfortable, judging by her wide smile. "You're so kind. But Mummy and I would like to see absolutely everything in my size ten. We believe in keeping an open mind until I've tried various styles, yeah?"

Denise was true to her word. She lost no time in ploughing her svelte way through half of the selection when Tracy, my next customer, arrived with her mother.

"And how are we tonight?" I greeted them with the customary pleasantries.

"Aye, wir doin' ok. Gaspin' tae see yir froacks. Ma pal Senga goat hers last year at yir shoap up the street and it wis jist bootiful, so it wis."

This was reassuring praise indeed. So when in Rome….

"Well," I held up a water silk beauty in her size sixteen, "how about this wee number. Eh? Fancy givin' it a go?"

Tracy looked joyfully at her mother. "Oh, my Goad! That's a smasher, inn't it Ma? Ah jist cannae wait tae see it oan."

"Right, get your kit off. Here we go."

Having placed the dress and other essentials about Tracy's person I seized the opportunity to zip to the other side of the screen and check Denise's progress. She had a petite figure and was a smidgen over five feet, so the gown she was wearing not only cascaded around her ankles, it was totally the wrong size and style for her frame.

"A tad overwhelming perhaps," her mother said with a little laugh.

Denise agreed. "Yeah, for sure. I had to allow myself a little giggle at this one." She pointed to the hanging rail, groaning with an overload of satin and lace. "May I see the lace empire line sitting at the back there. It looks very striking."

"Certainement," I responded and released the prize from its zipped polyester cover. "This is a Nella McCrapner creation. Such a beautiful fabric of Swiss guipure lace with a glorious bias cut skirt."

"Oh! How tres jolie," Denise agreed, determined not to be outdone bilingually as I helped her on with the gown.

It looked a promising prospect so I left the two purring over the dress, now paired with a stunning pillbox cap saturated with crystals.

I had no need to worry about Tracy who was having the time of her life self-accessorizing the moiree dress which she had obviously set her sights on. It is as much of a challenge to complement a dress with veil and headdress as it is finding the gown itself, but mother and daughter were managing well, happy to go back and forth trying long veils, short bouffant veils, tiaras and garlands. My lack of space and help at that time demanded that customers had to occasionally self serve. Did she really want this dress? I had to know if it was a waste of time to try even more accessorizing.

"Waant it? Ah cannae bear tae take it aff!" As if to prove the point, a little tear of happiness trickled down her pink cheek and I had to agree that the gown was amazing on her. But the long, dark hair hanging over her shoulders looked a bit untidy.

"The wedding ring collar neckline on this one will look much better with your hair up. Do ye' no' think so?" I chummied, as I lifted her hair up and back with one of the haircombs I kept for such a purpose.

"Ah know whit ye're sayin'," she agreed, glancing happily into the full length cheval mirror. "And ah'll hiv plenty o' time tae practice the herrdo – the weddin's six months fae noo."

"That'll dae it." I was absolutely falling into the vernacular now. I had to stop myself, as I popped back to Denise, from asking, "Hullawrerr. How's it gaun?"

Denise was feeling triste. "I have to confess I'm not experiencing the buzz from this dress at all. And I know I should. May I try on some more? "

I liberated another not-quite-so-high-end dress from its plastic prison and draped it onto the bride. Her smile as I zipped her up told it all. This was probably the one. So much for poor old Nella McCrapner's haute couture.

Haute couture….on the other side of the screen the customers were more interested in hot pies and chips.

"Nae point in wastin' any more o' yir time," Tracy told me happily as I popped my head around. "Ah jist love this yin and ah'm hivvin' it." She looked slightly embarrassed. "But could we jist gi' ye the deposit and leave? Ah've jist came fae ma work so I could eat a scabby horse and we'd like tae get oota here afore the chip shop shuts."

"Noo…I waant this wee short veil wi' the butterflies oan it and this tarara fur ma herr, tae," as she casually handed back the finest example of my Swarovski crystal tiaras. I wrote down the order posthaste not wishing to deprive her of her black pudding and chip supper.

"Cheerio the noo," was her final adieu to me as I turned back to deal exclusively with Denise. Thankfully, things were going well there, too.

"Just adore this little number and we think this is the one. Right, Mummy?" She must have noticed the deafening silence suddenly emanating from the other side of the screen. "I take it your other client has left, yeah?"

I responded with: "Aye, she his left, right enough. Whit a rerr terr all this is, eh?"

Then I gulped. How gauche! I realized I had used the wrong lingo with the wrong client and scolded myself silently. Bi-demographically, of course.

"Bejeez, my patter's like waatter. N'est ce pas?"

The Nappies Are Under the Tiaras

Doorbell rings. It's a Groundhog Day moment for me since the scenario is almost always the same. "Is this the house that has the bridal hire? Can we come in now or do we have to make an appointment?"

This was a daily occurrence and I wasn't even seeking out customers. No advertising, networking, nothing. Besides it was hard to network when the only people I seemed to talk to on a vaguely business level were the milkman, the postman and the 'green lady', the postnatal health nurse who dropped by occasionally to check on new mothers and their babies. There was no social media at that time, of course. So I was fairly confined with three very young children and wondering how on earth people were sourcing me.

Now, I absolutely WANTED to do business, but only the kind that fell into my lap. I suppose I was afraid I wouldn't be able to handle a bridal overload for although I had the front room set up nicely, I knew it was never going to be a suitable situation in the long term. That was another perplexity. For me, long term meant WHAT? Until the children were at school? Yonks away at that time. And where was I going with this tulle-clad King Kong of an enterprise, boldly trampling huge pearl and lace-gloved paws all over my already overcrowded domestic space? So many people nowadays, not just women, work from home – pandemics aside. That is great. Sitting in a living room doing computer work is one thing. My rather messy line involved inviting parties of bustling, chattering women in to the front area of my home, only to hope they would not notice the household holy chaos going on at the back.

No, my large and imposing front lounge was just not large and imposing enough for me most of the time. Yes, I had started the bridal hire at home in the flat but there had been no children then. I could afford the space – and it was peaceful. Now the pressing problem was proximity. There I would be, the ostensibly elegant saleslady showing off her delicious dresses and spouting off about the beauty of the cowl neckline, when suddenly there is an interruption. Kind of like this.....

A man's voice is heard behind the faint, hesitant knock at the door. I excuse myself and pop into the big t-shaped hallway to discuss with Other Half our latest domiciliary drama.

"I can't find the baby shampoo anywhere..."

"I already bathed the children and the baby, why...."

"I know that but I need to do it again. The little guy's hair is covered in chocolate Nutella and he's put it all over his sister, too. I think the baby's alright...." He seems a trifle unsure.

"Okay," I whisper, trying to be calm. "There's a fresh bottle in the big bathroom cupboard on the bottom shelf where I keep fresh supplies, right?"

He still looks hesitant about something. "Right. And you've moved the nappies. Where...?"

"Sorry. I forgot to tell you I've moved them into the linen cupboard in the utility room but I still have to sort it all properly. Maybe, tomorrow. Anyway, you're sure to see them. The nappies are all freshly washed and folded, right under that new box of tiaras...."

Of course I was certain that this had all been overheard by my customers. I felt my professional image was eroding nightly although I cannot actually recall any negative comments from clients. If anything they seemed amenable to it all, even to the sounds of baby and toddler tantrums. Daytime appointments were not an option for me since affordable daycare at that time was extremely rare and I understand it is still a challenge – even today with so many working mums. So I was stuck with evenings and my daytime working brides took full advantage of it.

The front room location did not have to be endured for long, thankfully. Pretty soon my private, exclusive, self-contained bridal salon was on its way when we eventually decided to convert and extend our unused garage. We had plenty of driveway space – which would come in useful a little later on for storing limousines – so this was not a sacrifice at all. It took several months to do the conversion work and I was champing at the bit to get some proper business space of my own, but it was so worth it! It was one big space catering to one group at a time, but that was fine, for now I had the best of both worlds. I could be close to the family nest but not TOO close. Well, I was at least twenty nappies, twelve baby baths and moderately a couple of Silver Cross prams away now. Things were looking up.

I stretched out many an evening with two or three appointments, and often we bashed on till midnight. It was a relief that the house was detached and a generous distance from both our neighbours, for there were only two other houses besides us. Other than them we were on a main route but surrounded by leafy parks and green fields at front and rear. This was just as well when a high spirited group of chattering females left my little salon at midnight like a bunch of merry Cinderellas.

I had a lot of fun at this rather odd location but importantly, I was able to juggle both business and domestic without major sacrifice. The setup served me well for the few years before all three children were in school, but ultimately I waved goodbye to the cozy home layout and found spacious premises – again in the town centre.

Although this new shop was on the first floor it came with the benefit of a downstairs shop window, invaluable for showing off the glamourous gowns to passing shoppers and the constant traffic on its main route. Almost immediately into this location our speciality, The Package Wedding was born. Since the latest move, I had sought to constantly widen the range of wedding services for clients, so the Package was just a natural evolvement. I had extended the services from merely dress hire to flowers, cars, cakes and photographers at the last shop, but now I moved on to selling dresses, providing gents' hire and introduced videographers, invitations, guest coaches et all. If a client signed up for a full wedding with the package, they received all these services discounted AND with free wedding management, naturally. I watched carefully over all the proceedings and experience enabled me to advise brides and grooms accordingly.

I needed staff to help me with all this new business and Marlon became one of them. He began work almost immediately in the new location to take over gents' hires of kilts and suits, but he was also invaluable for ladies' fittings, since he was a dab hand with a sewing needle. We found out to our delight and distress that he was also a clever baker. The first morning he started, he arrived with a zesty lemon meringue pie.

"Nice for a cup of tea at the break," he said. "I baked it myself and you'll love it."

We certainly did. Jinty, Maureen and I tucked in gleefully while Marlon excused himself with his tea mug to go outside for a ciggie. We had wondered why he wasn't having any delicious pie.

"Och, it is gorgeous. But it's put pounds on my hips something chronic. I'm on a strict diet the now. You'll never tempt me to eat THAT...."

This launched a long, joyous working relationship with Marlon whom we subsequently discovered was ALWAYS on a diet. For some reason he kept baking those cakes and bringing them in so all of us could get fat, bar himself. Except for Marlon, the rest of us could resist anything except temptation, sadly.

Maureen, my main assistant, was a forty-something plump and cheery saleswoman who could also 'fix a frock' and latterly her daughter Jennifer joined us periodically during the busy periods of summer weddings during her college holidays. Jinty was quieter and more serious and thankfully always realized that the success of our weddings was paramount. She had worked for a large city bridal store but had been disenchanted with their customer priority. She certainly helped us to hold our end up with clients, always putting their interests to the fore.

We managed in this upstairs rented location for several years with great success. It was beginning to feel a tad tight at the end and I was already half-looking for larger premises, probably on the fringes of the town. I felt that as a specialist type of business we had no strong need to be right smack in the middle of Coatbridge town centre. People could find us easily enough on the outskirts, and perhaps we could enhance our services even more with the extra space a move would allow us. The deed was finally done and the decision made for us thanks to our landlord, the town's local authority. They informed me they were doubling the rent and left us no choice but to either pay up or leave. I made an effort to buy the shop but was told that their policy was NEVER to sell their stock.

I found an old schoolhouse on the west side of the town and we converted it to pleasant, spacious, high profile premises incorporating a huge salon and with excellent disabled access. This was to be our final destination for the business and it was certainly a good move.

It is noteworthy that after we left the upstairs shop the local authority never did manage to rent it out again. It lay vacant, cold and neglected and eventually became a damp ruin. It lies there still, in serious disrepair, a monument to poor decision making by those who govern, the powers-that-be.....

The old first floor shop was ALMOST perfect for our purposes but there were a couple of minor drawbacks. One was the inside stairs. It was a bit of a bind to schlepp gowns in long covers, heavy menswear and other items down to a customer's car parked on the street – if they managed to find a parking spot at all. Of course, we were lucky to have ANY parking downstairs. In a town centre situation, this was a huge advantage. But those stairs! In reverse, some of our hire clients had the undiluted joy of lugging returned hired goods back up the wretched things.

Another negative feature of the upstairs shop's location was - embarrassment. We shared the building with another business whose inside door was right across the landing from ours. The irony was that their business was quite inapposite to ours. The whole situation verged on the ridiculous. I discovered just how ridiculous when I arrived at the shop extra early one October morning…..as you will find out in the next chapter.

For Sale – Fairy Tales and Pipe Dreams?

I had just congratulated myself on being so early to the salon. So early that all parking places outside were available, a rare thing indeed and as I nabbed one, I noticed her sitting on the step. Sitting on the cold, uncaring concrete slab of a step leading to our upstairs first floor shop. Her eyes were red rimmed and tired and her weary gaze seemed to only partly absorb the two bubbly young children who were hopping around her. Several large plastic shopping bags were scattered around the step and the front shop window. The bags had clearly been hastily filled with clothes and toys and appeared to be, for now at least, all the wordly goods of this little group. Such a lacklustre, lethargic woman contrasted dramatically with our striking, glittering, romantic window display flaunting fluffy gowns and satin ring pillows. The stuff of dreams. Sadly, I had already surmised that she was not to be a fairytale-seeking customer.

It was a nippy October morning and not yet eight o'clock. I had planned an early kick-off to a busy day but I hadn't anticipated this – then again neither had she. As I approached the large locked external double doors jangling my keys, she looked up at me and asked "Are you the lady from the Women's Aid? I need to see someone about my situation."

The location of our salon at that time was in the heart of the town centre. I had been there for over a year at this point, having finally broken ties with the business annex attached to my home, just a mile or so away. I had successfully bid on the lease of a first floor spacious office which served us well as a large, open plan salon. The fact that it was upstairs would, realistically, not have been acceptable if it hadn't been for the ground floor window included in the deal. It was a bonus showcase for us to sell our beautiful wares. The shop really was a good move in every sense, except for the fact that shortly after we moved in a women's shelter office was established in the adjacent premises, right across the stairwell from us. Ironic? Yes, indeed. To complete an unlikely trio, a couple of doors down in the same building

thrived a law firm who specialized in family law –
in other words, divorce.

So there we were peddling Cinderella fairytales
while the other occupants of our building were
acting as back up when the bubbles burst. Now I
believe I've been blessed with a sense of humour,
but I never could jest to our clients "Well, it's
great that your wedding went swimmingly. Now
if you have any problems later, just remember the
address because we have domestic abuse facilities
across the hall and if it gets really bad, we have
legal dissolution next door." I mean, how could
you joke about something like that? However the
absurdity of such a paradox did strike the odd
client who entered the premises, because
occasionally some wag, usually a male, would
offer a ripping remark.

Our doorstep resident looked to be in her early
thirties and the mother of the four year-old girl
and two year-old boy who were with her. Her
circumstances had obviously not made allowances
for fashion sense, since her appearance seemed to
prove that she had just grabbed clothes and
shoved them on. Her hair was dark blonde and
had seen a hair salon recently, that much I was
sure. But just then she was uncoordinated,
unkempt and probably uncaring. She had a nice
face – even with the dark circles, red eyes and tear

stains, you could tell she was pretty. Whatever
had happened, she had bolted from her home in a
big, big hurry. Her appearance and the badly
packed shopping bags told that tale. The children
were different. They had smart, matching anoraks
and trews and the oversized pompoms on their
wooly hats bopped around as they ran up and
down the pavement laughing and playing. In any
other circumstance they would have been a cute
distraction. Just not today. Thankfully, they
seemed to be cozily unaware of the sad scenario
around them and the distress of their mother. I
mentally shelved the notion that disruption was
something they were used to.

After explaining that I had the bridal shop upstairs
she was invited to come up for a cup of tea and a
chat. "The Women's Aid won't be open for about
an hour. You'll be fine waiting in our shop." I
lifted as many of the bags as I could, leaving her
to take the rest and manage the children.

I put the kettle on and opened some biscuits for
the wee ones. We had a box of toys tucked away
for emergencies with bored kids, so I dragged it
out of the storeroom and concentrated on their
mum. It was heartbreaking to see her distress, her
confusion about what had brought her to this
point. She told me her name was Anna and as she
spoke, her words came out in incoherent spurts

and chokes. She struggled to speak, thwarted by tears and emotion as she tried to explain to me why she was here. It was as if she was justifying her exodus from the marital home, dragging her kids out into the cold October dawn. Anna was clearly desperate to open up emotionally and through tearful outpourings I caught the gist of her story.

"I just had to get out of there, last night was the last straw and he finally broke me." She explained the buildup to her problems, shaking as she held on to her cup with both hands.

"I can't take any more of the bullying – its not just once in a while – it's constant. I'm a bag of nerves just thinking of his coming home from work at night. My heart sinks when I hear the door opening, wondering what he's gonna pick for a fight next. It could be anything. He might not like his dinner or the kids are annoying him – or there's a fly on the wall. I don't understand it. I've tried to be a good wife and support him and take care o' things – all the household stuff, you know…" She broke down for a while, anguishing over the issues.

"I've told myself maybe it's me. He's just sick of me now. He's told me I'm useless, no good or help to him. He could be right. Lately I've no

heart for anything – things I used to care about.
Except the kids. The weans have to come first
after all. My life might be over, but theirs has to
go on."

I could do nothing for her other than listen. It
seemed all I could do was pour out more tea and
keep offering biscuits.

"He used to be fine. WE used to be fine – and
then a couple of years ago he went into business
with his brother-in-law. A building business. He
seems to be doing ok with it – he never actually
speaks to me right so it's hard to say. But I don't
think money's an issue. It's awful that I don't
even know all this stuff, but he just shuts me out.
It's like I'm nobody."

"But I know that since he started working for
himself, he's never off my back. I can do
nothing right and the kids are beginning to sense
it..." She broke down completely at the thought
of the children and I couldn't help crying with
her. I did want to be strong, to simply sympathize
but it was difficult not to feel her pain. There
were parts of her account, the business and the
lack of money worries, which could have sounded
like a success story. But it was the complete
opposite.

"It's not worth it, the business and more money. None of that matters when you're miserable, when your man can't spend time, doesn't WANT to spend time with your weans. He's too busy screaming at me to even bother with the kids, but last night they were crying too, and scared. He started at tea time and was still going in the wee small hours. It was a nightshift of fighting and screaming. I got the kids to bed finally and it was hard to lift them and take them with me this morning. It was still dark when we left. They looked so content in their wee beds. But I had to get out of there and I couldn't leave my weans. Never, ever."

Strangely, in the middle of her sobs she half smiled. "I think he's losing it. He never gives the kids the time of day, it's like they don't exist. But this last few weeks he keeps on about getting a dog. A dog! He's like a wee selfish, spoiled boy at times. But the dog would be treated the same as us eventually. Ignored at best…."

Her tragic sobbing should have alerted the children to her side but no, they still played happily on the salon floor drinking milk and gobbling biscuits. Perhaps they were used to Mummy's tears or hopefully they were childishly and innocently immune.

Was this man physically abusing her, I asked. I think I already knew the answer since there didn't seem to be a mark on her face, no bumps or bruises. Besides, she would not be headed to Women's Aid, it would have been an ambulance or taxi to the hospital – and the police would have been involved too.

"No, he threatens to hit me but he never does. Takes it out on the doors and the furniture. Last night he broke all the good dinner set my mother got me as a wedding present." Rueful smile here. She looked at me soulfully as if she wanted me to agree with her next statement.

"I sometimes wish he would give me a good thump and get it over with. Maybe I could take that, but the endless swearing, nagging and criticism - he calls me vile names in front of the weans – it's not a way to live, not a way to live…."

I found out that there were quiet spells occasionally.

"Maybe – every couple of weeks maybe – he'll clam up. I call it going into a dark hole, 'cos that's what it's like. He doesn't speak at all to me or the kids. He won't eat or make demands. He just freezes up and its as if the rest of us don't exist." She had a glimmer of a smile about all this.

"A lot of women would be spooked out but I'm just glad to get peace for a wee while when that happens. It never lasts for long, more's the pity. Before you know it, he's off again, torturing the house wi' his ranting and raving."

I could only offer an ear, encouraging her to talk and get it all out of her system. At one point she went to the bathroom and came back looking marginally better. She had splashed her face with cold water and tidied her hair. The pink tee shirt she had been wearing inside out was now turned the right way, so I desperately hoped that was a good sign.

Eventually we both heard the adjacent office unlock their door for business so I went across the hall to pop my head in and alert them about their potential new client. Within five minutes Anna was in there and probably going through the same scenario for the second time. I had had the full dramatic dress rehearsal and found it truly draining. From then on I had massive respect for that Women's Aid office. To have to deal with woeful tales like this each day, some much worse and involving physical and mental abuse, made me sick to my stomach.

I thought about Anna's situation, how difficult it really was. Because there was no apparent physical abuse, she just might have been a non-urgent case. I am speculating because I really don't know the boundaries of cases like this. What was troublesome to me was the knowledge that there are many women in similar circumstances who, because their faces and bodies happen to be bruise free, are not seen as victims. But it doesn't mean the trauma and torture of mental abuse can't destroy a woman, a mother's life. And her children's lives, too.

"I sometimes wish he would give me a good thump and get it over with…."

Suffice to say that for the rest of that very busy day I found it extremely tough to sell our Disney-esque dreams after witnessing Anna's heartbreak. Her tearstained face kept haunting me. It haunts me to this day.

In Vino Veritas

The Reverend Luke Warren was in a fighting mood. He frowned, glared at me for a few seconds and was obviously making a supreme effort to compose himself. Nonetheless I had to battle on to make him see that I was right, that I was a spokesperson, in a sense, for this bride.

In my finest sergeant major voice I declared, "So you just have to agree Mr. Warren that the flowers in the church MUST go next to the communion table….there IS no other suitable place."

I turned away from him slightly dismissively and glanced around the little Victorian church. It was simple and serene and to be honest needed nothing much to embellish it. But there was to be my client's wedding here in just over a week - and it was a given that there would be flowers on the dais just below the charming oak pulpit – fragrant roses, lilies and gypsophila arranged artistically to outline for all the guests that this was indeed a celebration, a new beginning - a big deal! I would not give up the fight, no sir.

The dignified clergyman was not a man to be trifled with. But then again the truth was that very few ministers and priests were absolutely compliant when it came to wedding planning. They had opinions on the placement of flowers, the location in the church of the videographer and photographer, if indeed they were allowed in at all and whether there should be pew ends in the church. The Warren attitude was familiar to me. When it came to wedding organization I was a one woman army – it seemed like I was regularly combatting the cause of some poor bride who simply wanted nothing more than a dream-wedding.

Rev. Warren was definitely top of the field in objecting. He was the original cleric colonel, on a mission and steeped in the traditions of the church. He turned to me and tossed out an effective grenade.

"I will be here to oversee these decorations next week," he fired back at me, guns blazing, "I must be present in the church for other matters and whilst I am here I will not shirk my duty to ensure everything is executed as….discussed." He enunciated this last word to make it sound like 'disgust'. Perhaps I was being a tad sensitive. No, I could swear his grey moustache bristled as he spoke. The minister would have been about sixty, a few years short of retirement and the promise of a hopefully peaceful life free of pesky wedding organizers like me. I thought I had better quit whilst I was ahead. I was beginning to feel the effects of battle fatigue.

"Thank you sir. Now I must be off to the reception venue to check the setup for floral requirements and other matters to do with this wedding at the Loch View Rooms. Fiona Ross has very definite ideas about the layout there, too. This is what I'm trying to make you see. You know her well so you can understand her expectations, yes?"

Uh, uh. There was that frown again. Please, no more battle cries. And I had almost made it to the vestry door, too. Just slightly wounded.

He explained his perplexity. "I simply don't understand young Fiona choosing the Loch View Rooms for her wedding reception. Why, I have known that little lady since she was here in Sunday School. I offered her the church hall, but she refused it. It's a lovely big space." He was clearly dismayed at this rejection so I offered clarification.

"Mr. Warren, the Durwall Parish Church Hall would be adequate in size and location." Yes, even I could employ tact if needs be. "But you don't allow alcohol there! What kind of wedding would it be if there were to be no champagne, beer or wine? You can hardly blame the bride for her choice."

My wicked, secret twin Ursula was rearing her feisty little head again. Ursula did show up at the most inopportune moments, her temper almost demanding to be restrained because I really had to stop fighting causes that weren't even part of my remit. Didn't I have enough on my wedding plate just swaying him on the flowers, videos and photos? I should leave the merits and demerits of booze to the vicar.

He came back with the ultimate coup. " Well I don't understand that at all. When you have the spirit of the Lord then other spirits seem unnecessary." He spoke quietly and thoughtfully, his expression having softened since our previous exchange regarding the flowers.

"I'll uplift the flowers on the Monday morning Mr. Warren, after Fiona's Saturday wedding," I added to the fray as a change of strategy. This was my usual game plan after a weekend wedding at Warren's church. The regular congregation attending Sunday Services seemed to enjoy the novelty of wedding flower arrangements still in situ so there was no rush to uplift. Afterwards, however, the minister wanted all signs of that wedding gone. Completely obliterated. He always insisted they be taken to a nearby care home whilst inferring all the while that this was an act of unselfish kindness.

This time was to be different. I was certain because the frown reappeared again. "No, no! I have to tell you we are inviting some of the fathers from St Paul's Catholic Church that Sunday. They will be sharing the dais with me so we will require more space than usual. The flowers must be gone by then." He absolutely noted my surprise at his words, for he hesitated and then quickly added, "It is quite a feat for our parish to succeed in involving another denomination into our fellowship. These ecumenical accomplishments are very significant." After some mild congratulations, I agreed that I would have the church cleared of the dreaded flowers by Saturday evening instead.

As I drove away from the church I reflected that Luke Warren was not a progressive thinker, so this effort to accommodate a Catholic denomination was unexpected. St. Paul's was only a mile or so away and was already part of the community, but bringing two religious sects together here, in the west of Scotland was no mean feat. Nonetheless I admired his principles and enthusiasm. As for his other enthusiasm for alcohol-free weddings, that was never going to work. I could not help laughing out loud just thinking about it. He was truly convinced that a booze-free bash would come off. No champagne, wine or beer! I was hardly a hardened drinker myself, but even I shuddered at the thought.

A few days after this Susan Hill came into the salon. She was a potentially new client who wanted to discuss the entire wedding package so I chose to go over the ropes with her myself. Unfortunately, she was alone with no mum, no sister, no groom, no bridesmaids. Generally this meant no immediate booking either. Few brides acted solo in making vital wedding plans, for moral support was everything and a friend or sister was usually invaluable. Booking was a big step and a wedding was not cheap, so you couldn't blame a new client for taking their time, talking to friends or family and being comfortable with the decision.

However, Susan was very serious about the package deal and explained why. Although she originally lived locally she was now based in the Isle of Wight with her fiancé which meant she would not have a lot of opportunity to run from pillar to post on trips to her mother's home, arranging various services. Our business bundle was ideal for her. I ran through everything we provided from the dresses to the invitations, and a few side dishes to boot, such as limos, flowers, cake, videographer, photographer, men's tuxedos or kilts, beauty therapy, and so on and so on. All a couple had to do with this one was find the church and the reception. We took care of the rest. This was a taste of ambrosia for busy people as our regular team provided the services and there was one bill, one phone call, one business place to visit. We were the original one-stop-shop. In other words you could let us have the nervous breakdown and go home and put the kettle on - or even better, open a bottle of wine._

Susan wanted to go home and open that bottle of wine. It was a relief for her to book so many aspects of her big day in one fell swoop. She would need help, but we just did not realize how much at that point in our new relationship. She was resolute. "I want to book the package. We can choose dresses in a few months, but the main thing is we will have no gaps. The brunt of the wedding will be done and when I go back to Isle of Wight tomorrow, I'll be able to rest easy."

I was happy she had shown faith in us. A friend had recommended us to her and this was always the best type of positive business. I pulled out our diary. This was in the early nineties before we used computers. I checked the details. "The wedding is in August next year, right? Date? Oh, the 14th of August…" I could see this was a busy weekend but we were not fully booked yet. Susan was smiling in a relieved way. I had seen smiles like hers a million time before. It was a strangely wistful smile brides would engage when they took care of wedding business. It was a smile of contentment, of stress and anxiety erased, a special smile that said, 'right, now I have passed the baton to you, hurrah!'

"Which church or location?" I probed further. The answer was St Paul's. "St Paul's right here in town, right?" Yes again. Strange…. "And the time of the ceremony?" I asked a little hesitantly. The answer I was dreading actually materialized. She stated it would be three o'clock. Dear, dear.

I took a deep breath before explaining. Looking back, I should have offered her a drink and told her to stay calm.

"Well…we have, and have had for over four months, a 3 o'clock wedding there in that church on the same date. I hate to say it but you've been double booked by St Paul's." Susan's wistful little smile had faded. So too, it seemed, had the bright sunshine outside. It was suddenly grey and overcast. The poor girl was in tears.

"I don't know what to do. I've booked my hotel, they have no other suitable dates and what about the holidays from work for me and Gavin for the wedding and honeymoon….it's disastrous! Oh, God help me! And I'm not here to deal with it when I go back to England!" _____

I had to offer some escape and rescue plan by thinking quickly. "Look, go back to your life down south. Leave it with me. I'll go see the fathers at St Paul's myself. Perhaps we can reshape times a little bit. Remember the other bride is our client too so she might work with us and consent to a wee bit of a time change."

This was more optimism than conviction. Messing with a wedding that had been neatly set in its own little frame was very dodgy. Brides could have nervous breakdowns. Even wedding planners could have nervous breakdowns.

"Now which priest did the booking for you? Oh, Father O'Rourke. Right, I'll phone you after I've sorted it out. I'm sure it'll be fine. Remember we've got many advantages as both weddings are in our hands and we've also got fifteen months in our pockets. Susan, time is on our side!" God, I was good. Susan had just freshly booked us and was already witnessing, even at this early stage, the value of one stop planning.

She left looking slightly more reassured and I began to focus on the whole business more clearly. Was I overstepping the mark by jumping into the fray? Our work usually started AFTER the church and hotel were solidly booked. This was not our remit. Perhaps it was not my responsibility, but I felt I could possibly douse the flames of furor better than some 'too close for comfort' family members. I knew from experience that weddings are breeding grounds for irrational and emotive behavior from families. Let the professional stranger try first.

I refused to bank Susan's deposit cheque till things were settled. But what a curious thing to happen. Looking back on it now, amazingly this was the only time we were ever confronted with such a situation, before or afterwards and we were involved in thousands of weddings. After all, how tough can it be for anyone, especially in this one-off, one chance to get it right business, to open a diary and check a date? And yet it was certainly serendipitous for the bride, too. I thought of the old movie 'Casablanca' and the classic line for anyone who enjoys the film noir era. As Humphrey Bogart famously uttered: "Of all the gin joints in all the world, she had to walk into mine!" Yes, Susan had been unlucky in one way but her angels had been with her latterly. She had chosen us. We had picked up on the problem before (we hoped) it was too late. I fervently prayed I was not entering yet another battlefield with the local clergy, but the matter couldn't be ignored.

The following morning found me driving into the pristine courtyard at St. Paul's Church. My earlier phone call to Father O'Rourke had been received with curiosity but I had no desire to bemire the situation over the telephone. Some business, like this business, merited an eyeball to eyeball meeting even if some of my frequent associations with the ecclesiastical had left me a little wary. I was sure that forewarned was forearmed, and I selfishly wanted all the advantages in any ensuing heated discussion. I pulled my car behind the huge modern church and noted how clean, organized and tidy the whole place was - including the parish house, where the priests resided. Things seemed to be very pristine and organized on the outside, at least….

As I walked up to the door it opened before I had a chance to even place my finger on the bell. The housekeeper? No, it was a tall, gangly and slightly stooped elderly priest who had evidently been keeping note of my arrival since I had driven into the parish grounds. "Father O'Rourke?" I vaguely recognized the gentleman but had not seen him for several years. I prided myself on knowing most of the clergy in the area due to the nature of my business, not on my piety, and the priest was just almost familiar. Names were sometimes jumbled for me, but I always remembered faces and as I fought my way through the mists of memory I recollected that he had already retired, hence his absence these past few years.

Fr O'Rourke invited me into a spacious library delightfully busy with books. There was a pleasant calming composure in the room that I felt was rather at odds with the personality now standing in front of me. Because that was the problem, he was not standing so much as wobbling. I wondered if he felt unwell but he was not at all pale. In fact he was very red in the face. My senses caught a sniff of spirits as he came close to me to usher me into a comfortable leather reading chair. No…it couldn't be....! It was barely midmorning and I personally hadn't had even a cup of tea. Then I glimpsed a little silver tray perched on an adjoining side table. Pride of place on this stood a large bottle of whisky, or rather a large HALF FULL bottle of whisky. Two crystal glasses accompanied the bottle. One of them had been used already for I could clearly spy a dinner mint's depth of golden nectar still surreptitiously soiling the bottom of the glass. I was beginning to understand how the double booking had happened.

I explained to the veteran priest our dilemma, about which he seemed a little embarrassed. His soft Irish accent was almost as charming as the man himself.

"Well, you see I don't usually take the wedding bookings, Father Foley and Father Byrne are more active now than I am since they are much younger." He rolled his eyes a little and ran his fingers through a generous mane of silvery hair before going on. "I'm supposed to be retired but you could say I've become a substitute or stand in priest for the parish." This was why I hadn't seen him for some time.

He sat down on the adjacent leather chair right next to the little whisky-laden table. "They haven't put me out to graze yet, so I'm grateful for that. The both of them, the young fellas, just left on business to Scots College in Rome so I'm in charge for a few days and I was the one who took this wedding booking last week. Not doing much of a job, now. Am I?" He bowed his head and placed both hand palms in the prayer position as if to beg my forgiveness.

He was trying to lighten the moment but as he looked up again I could see the perplexity on his rosy, lined face. His vulnerability was showing which made it hard to feel badly towards him so I reassured him that I would be willing to attempt to tidy the situation with our two clashing brides if he would agree to comply with a new revised schedule.

"Of course, of course, whatever it takes," he assured me, looking not a little relieved. "You look like a strong assertive woman, indeed you do! Where would we be now without our good womenfolk?" I offered some solutions to our dilemma with new times and other strategies. There was to be no battle on this front. I contentedly imagined him waving and flaunting his imaginary white flag for all to see. So far, so good.

Father O'Rourke was obviously relieved, too. He stretched out his arms to me in a gesture of solidarity and declared, " That's grand. Just grand. Now would you like to join me in a wee sip of something to celebrate the saving of the day, as it were?" He leaned over the drinks tray and picked up the whisky bottle. Impulsively, I stood up quickly to leave, not trusting myself not to bash on about the dangers of being incapacitated during the business day, for I was sure that his half full bottle, or possibly another totally empty bottle, had been the culprit in all this. The clinking of these pretty crystal glasses had caused a bit of emotional pain and a fair bit of rearrangement work for a good many people. But there was little use in hammering such a fact home to this affable member of St. Paul's clergy.

"No thank you, Father," I said firmly. "I have lots to do today – and I'm driving." My nerves had been rattled with all this and I was a little jealous of his nonchalant, complaisant attitude. I was probably more than a little jealous too, of his relaxed, more committed relationship with the whisky bottle. At that moment I should have loved a nice whisky with ice and lemon...so I mentally promised myself one later, much later. Perhaps after I had had that cup of tea, or perhaps later tonight when all this was done.

I contacted bride one, Amelia. There was not a nervous breakdown in sight when I went over to her home early that evening to share the dubious tidings face to face. In fact she and her fiance stayed almost unnaturally calm. The reality was it was still over a year to the wedding so the exact hour of the ceremony was not that vital at this stage and would involve little inconvenience. But considering she had not been acquainted with Susan personally, I thought she reacted kindly and considerately. We discussed the possibility of her wedding being moved forward to two o'clock from its original three pm. Then the second wedding, Susan's wedding, could proceed at four instead of three o'clock. For Catholic weddings with a lengthy mass a generous interval was essential between ceremonies. The couple tossed some ideas around then agreed quickly and goodnaturedly.

The reality was that the better side of this deal was landing in Amelia's lap because the earlier the wedding ceremony, the better for all concerned. This would leave more time for photos and getting to the reception on time, more time for late coming guests. Any extra time up any nuptial sleeve was a bonus, believe me. Amelia and Dan were no fools and I had a hunch they were secretly delighted to push the time forward. Such a relief.

Now I would get back to Susan tonight, too. It was late, but I was sure she would want a phone call telling her the results of my efforts, although she had no other option but to come on board. Her later schedule of four o'clock meant that things could be tight, but with my company at the helm it would be easier to negotiate the ebb and flow of the wedding. She had been unsure about a location for photos after the ceremony. Often we would drive miles out of town to beauty spots to accommodate photographers, which took lots of time. I suggested a little quiet floral garden near to the church as a compromise. This in itself helped to make up a lot of the lost time. Our limo drivers and photography team would work expeditiously to create a happy, efficient timetable. This is when teamwork is invaluable – our little rep company would excel – we all knew each other, knew the ropes and we would deliver results. I have seen too many weddings where photographers, (not ours) and videographers (not ours) plus limo drivers (not ours) have all been at loggerheads with each other and complaining about the schedule during the proceedings. Each of these individual businesses seemed to care only about their particular remit, not in helping each other to achieve the best result for the wedding couple. These attitudes were sadly quite common but with the situation here, both weddings under our care, we could help control both schedules. Many years of experience had taught me that the

key factor to a successful wedding was timing –
and we had a masterplan this time!

Susan was a happy girl when I phoned her later
that night .

"I'm so relieved – now I can breathe easily
again," she said. "I'll call the reception tomorrow
and let them know about the time change. It
should all fall into place, thank goodness."

She added that being married in St. Paul's was
very important to her. "I've been going there
since I was a wee girl with my family. I know
Father O'Rourke is a bit old and dozy now, but I
never thought he could mess up like this."

I refrained from giving her the lowdown of his
frequent tipples. The main thing was, we were
back on track.

Eventually, all the clients even gained a little
monetary advantage because of the clashings. I
realized it would be easier and cheaper to offer
both brides a shared church floral deal. And as
there would be no time to go in to St. Paul's to
change arrangements for each individual
ceremony, I recommended that both groups could
share the costs and we would blend their colours
of pink and blue together in one set of flowers.

This also applied to the pew ends. A not inconsiderable saving for them.

One year on The Big Day arrived and we prepared ourselves to be extra vigilant. The church proceedings for both parties ran smoothly thanks to our team. Of course, I was hovering around both goings on like a vigilant parent seeing their child off to first day at school. Guests had to be ushered a little more eagerly than normal, since they always seemed to want to hang around the church instead of getting onto the reception via the courtesy coach or whatever. Perhaps they just like to get fresh air, who knows, but we had to keep things moving along so that one wedding crowd didn't amalgamate into another unwittingly.

Finally, as the last guest jumped into the last coach headed for the last reception and as the last shred of confetti was being thrown into the last bridal limousine, a tall, cassock enshrouded figure was seen lingering outside the church portals of St. Paul's. Yes, it was Father O'Rourke clutching a very large broom and assiduously sweeping up the excess confetti in his path. Although he seemed a trifle unsteady he was obviously in a hurry, perhaps to get back into his study and that lovely little silver toddy tray.

Now let us go back to the previous year to my initial skirmish with the Rev Warren of Durwall Church. Shortly after this I came across him accidentally. He strolled, perhaps tottered is a better word, towards me one evening as I was walking our two little Yorkies in the park adjacent to my home. It was around nine o'clock, still daylight and the weather was warm and agreeable - as was the clergyman, which made a pleasant change.

"Hello, hello! Just taking a verdant short cut through the park back to my home, the church manse," he said as he attempted to kneel down towards the doggies. "I have had a most congenial evening - most congenial indeed!" He laughed without restraint and without any obvious reason to do so. He certainly seemed different and there was a strong whiff of alcohol about his person. I decided to give him the benefit of the doubt. I decided it was probably aftershave or men's cologne or some such thing but suddenly as he edged closer, I was forced to acknowledge that it was definitely alcohol. Whisky, even. Perhaps a fine peaty single malt. Certainly it reeked of a twelve year old one and probably from a Speyside distillery. Oh, no. There I was letting the situation run away with me again. Why, the Reverend Warren despised alcohol. Such a sauce would not soil his lips. And whisky no less! After all, this was the man who spurned the very idea of even a wedding offering the demon drink. This was a man whose strongest and only tipple would have been the watered down wine on offer at Sunday communion.

He proved once and for all, albeit he was a vicar, a man of the cloth, that indeed 'in vino veritas'. He turned away from the Yorkies and straightened up, a trifle uncertainly, whilst oozing an uncharacteristic bonhomie.

"You know how I have been actively emboldening our ecumenical efforts lately?"

I nodded, amazed and remembered his idealistic fraternization with the Catholic Church. Specifically St.Paul's.

"Well then," he paused for a brief hiccup, "you will recall our attempts to forge a union between Durwall Church and the good parish of St. Paul's?" There was a distinctive slurring of the vowels. "I must declare that I am most encouraged. Tonight I had a marvellous tete a tete with a member of the senior clergy at St. Paul's. The honourable Father O'Rourke – what an erudite and refreshing host!"

This was shortly after my initial meeting with the eccentric senior priest and his silver, trouble-laden drinks tray. I now knew why 'refreshing' was an apt choice of word.

He went on. "I feel quite intoxicated...." Another germane word choice. "Yes, intoxicated by the realization that we have common bonds, common bonds, by jove. We are both determined to nurture this alliance. Ecumenical union is the thing. Indeed it is." There followed a distinctive burp, after which he bid farewell and tottered unsteadily homewards.

I had no doubt that whilst nurturing the alliance, a great degree of hydration would have entered the process, too. But this was best left alone, for the Rev Luke Warren was now relaxed, elated and content. It was nice to see him smiling at me for a change with no battles between us about wedding protocol. Because of his libatious liaison with Father O'Rourke he was feeling victorious.

I decided I would end my dog walkies, go home and cheerfully drink to that.....

A Heatwave, Two Weddings and a Funeral

It was baking hot in the van as I headed back to the salon, tired and a wee bit irritated. There never seemed to be enough hours in the day just now right at the height of the wedding season, even with our whole team working at full stretch.

Much earlier that Friday I had been to Drums Hotel and Whitelaw Church helping our florists to finish in time for today's events. They were managing ok and everything looked great so I left them to get on with it. I had previously done the dirty work, into Glasgow flower market at 4o'clock that morning and had prepared flowers for the orders for today and the next to make things quicker for assembly. Making up bouquets and other arrangements was not the hard part for an experienced florist. The market run and preparation were the hard work, similar to many creative tasks - eighty per cent preparation, twenty per cent inspiration.

There had been much more running around helping out and doing checks, but now that we were all done with today's jobs, I had to work on tomorrow's. The Royal Hotel needed my attention for drop-offs. There was another wedding there today which limited the preparation, but I could still do deliveries, helping the pace for Saturday's arrangements and set-up. The hotel understood the pressures. They were part of the same pressure themselves and always allowed us a little cool room to store our floral and cake goodies for the following day.

Finally there were more floral duties to be done at St. Paul's in preparation for the same affair tomorrow which was almost totally under our auspices. Wasn't all this enough to sort out, I asked myself. So why did the girls insist I come back to the shop, why could they not handle this on their own...

I stormed into the salon to confront Maureen and Jinty. Marlon was out and about delivering kilt orders. These women were normally my rocks, never flinching under the incredible stress of producing complete weddings, putting out merchandise and dealing with clients' wedding nerves on a regular basis. This particular scenario however, seemed to sweep them into a cold sweat.

"What is going on here – this is just a dress sale like any other," I stage whispered, not even trying to hide my annoyance at being here at all. "I have to be at St. Paul's in an hour to get the flowers done for tomorrow and this is seriously screwing up my schedule!"

The poor ladies were like two nervous kittens. "We really can't do any more appointments like these," Jinty muttered, scarcely audible. "Remember we did two last week and three of them a fortnight before that. We can't keep this up, it's really upsetting my nerves! I wish Marlon was here! He's much better at this stuff…."

I shook my head in disgust. "I know he is, but our Marlon's too busy doing deliveries and helping to produce weddings for this weekend, remember? Ok, I'll take care of this myself, tight schedule or no…."

I had been resentful before, now I was exasperated. I pushed past both of them and made my way to the fitting rooms at the back of the salon. I could see three or four wedding gowns hanging on the rail outside cubicle four, our largest booth. The curtain was still open and our new customer was waiting patiently, perched awkwardly on the dainty little stool inside. I harnessed some composure quickly before it totally deserted me and apologized for the delay, indicating that I would be taking over the dress fitting.

"That's okay," I was told, "I'm in no hurry at all. I finished work early today so I'm good. Plenty of time." At this point I resisted the urge to check my watch. I wished I had plenty of time....

I explained that for dress try-ons, especially bridal gowns, an assistant had to be present at all times in order to protect our expensive stock. "So, what is your name?" I enquired as sweetly as I could muster.

"I'm Darren," he said. "All these dresses are in the sale, right? This is just for a fancy dress party so I don't want to spend too much money."

I told him I understood. Yes, I understood perfectly.

When gentlemen happened to come into the salon like this (according to my assistants there were zillions of them) to almost always look at our reduced rail of wedding gowns, the fancy dress party was always the occasion, apparently. I had no particular feelings about their motives for dress shopping. I considered the whole scenario pretty harmless. After all, as I told the girls, business was business – a sale was a sale.

Darren was a big strapping lad, aged about mid-thirties and wearing a smart grey business suit with dark leather loafers which he slipped off before the fitting for some unfathomable reason. Since he was not wearing foundation or lipstick – I had a quick close look to make sure – we did not require placing a fine voile square over his head and face to avoid makeup smudges. I stretched up to place the first dress over his head and bare chest, reflecting on how tall he was – over six-three in his bare feet. However, he did not have bare feet. As I glanced down towards our plushly carpeted floor I saw that he was wearing ladies tights. I zipped up the dress at the back and there was the waistband of the aforesaid pantyhose, protruding over the top of his slacks. All of which silently denied his proffered motive for being here. But I was not annoyed or shocked – actually, I thought that Darren had been better prepared for this fitting than most women. Occasionally I had to reprimand our female clients for coming unprepared for fittings without the proper bra or other underwear, but Darren had brought his tights, good lad.

We worked our way through the small number of dress offerings. Since Darren needed a size 20 at

112

least, and it had to be a reduced item, his choice was considerably narrowed. There were only two that suited and he liked both of them, trying on each in turn about three times. I did not hide my glancing at my watch this time….I had to get over to St. Paul's soon and spend a couple of hours there with the flowers. Then onto the Royal Hotel….my tummy was rumbling too, since I had had nothing to eat all day.

Finally Darren made his choice and I told the girls to wrap his purchases. I had even sold him a cute wee veil and headdress to complement his outfit. He had made a bit of a fuss choosing these items too, but he was extremely happy. Another satisfied customer, I thought, and surprisingly picky about a fancy dress party. I mulled over that we sometimes thought our lady clients were too finicky, but this gentleman was just as bad. Well, at least Darren never uttered the immortal words: 'Does my bum look big in this?'

When he left I got an earful from the staff. "I think it's just wrong and if we're not careful we'll soon have the reputation of being the transvestite wedding shop," moaned Maureen.

And from Jinty, who looked very serious and contemplative, "I don't think I could go in there and put a dress on him – I mean, he's a man! Did he keep his trousers on? My God if my Gerry thought I was in a cubicle alone with a bloke trying on stuff he would be absolutely livid." Then she seemed to do a mental flip as she thought more deeply about the scenario. "But if he was wearing a dress, maybe Gerry wouldn't mind so much, what do ye think?"

I was glad to leave and bash onto St. Paul's after going back to the workshop for my supply of flowers, greenery and the rest. It was difficult in this intense heat producing floral work. Every stem was so delicate and the storage conditions had to be shady and almost shivery, which it definitely was NOT in the van at this point. It was very early evening now and still twenty-nine celsius outside. The quicker this load was arranged in soaking wet oasis then placed in a cool, high ceilinged church, the better.

Father O'Rourke was standing on the steps of St. Paul's and looking a trifle impatient as he had a right to. I had guessed the church would be locked, for after all I was almost an hour later than arranged, his housekeeper had left and he was now in charge of allowing me entry. Nonetheless, he gallantly dismissed my apology. Yes, we were bonding.

"Don't worry about it at all. You're grand, just grand."

I was touched. "Father you should be sainted for waiting so long for me," I teased, "You have the patience of one, that's for sure."

"My parable for this evening is this - it's easy to have a warm heart on a warm evening when you are waiting with a cold beer! Come in through here," I grabbed a couple of boxes of flowers and followed him into the church house. We went down a confusing maze of corridors through the big, modern dwelling towards the internal entry to the church itself. I wasn't familiar with this means of access. Before I had used just the main doors of the church and I agonized whether I would be able to find my way back to the van to haul in the rest of the flowers and tools needed for the job. Right, left, turn here….It was quite complex and I was amusing myself with the thought that if only I had a slice of bread like Hansel and Gretel, I could leave a crumb trail. We finally stopped at a tiny scullery, just before the church access, but I persisted in glancing back over my shoulder trying to figure the way back to the van.

The elderly priest was more than gallant. He seemed to read my thoughts and offered to help me go back to lug the rest of my gear. As we grabbed some more stuff from the van I watched Father O'Rourke and thought how he seemed to be raising himself gracefully out of retirement these days. However, still fresh in my mind was the case of the double booking a few months earlier – an error by Father O'Rourke which, if it hadn't been for gobsmacking coincidence, enabling the salon to catch the mistake early, might have resulted in two disastrously clashed complete weddings for two of my own clients.

"Well this is a busy parish alright," he chatted away as he walked back to the scullery. "I do my little bit to help out. And what a weekend! There was a wedding today, your own client's tomorrow" – he threw open the workroom's big, groaning oak door leading to the church dais and altar – "and a funeral in the morning!"

I looked through the open door in horror at a shiny, brass-encrusted coffin reposing gloomily on two drab grey pedestals right in front of the altar. But how….I turned to the priest sharply. No time for niceties now, this was serious.

"You never mentioned a funeral when I phoned the other day to make arrangements for these flowers, Father." I had to stop for breath – and an excuse to shirk my duty. "So it's still okay to dress the church for the wedding? Normally in a situation like this we try to avoid a clash." Raised voice alert. "After all, sir – wedding flowers at a funeral?"

He looked at me smugly as if he had just won the cleric of the year award. "Well we can all pre-book weddings, but funerals are what happens to some people when they are busy making plans, you know?"

I was surprised to hear him quote John Lennon so fluently like this, but he was right. Funerals often interfered in our best laid plans for weddings although generally I was kept in the frame when interments were imminent.

He went on, "The widow Farrell doesn't mind the flowers being here at all – in fact she thinks it'll be a nice extra touch for poor Tommy here. She's a keen gardener, you know!" He nodded towards the coffin which seemed to be spookily occupying the whole front of the church where I would be working.

I stood dumbfounded, staring in shock at the ghoulish wooden box, with Father O'Rourke chattering on cheerfully as I only half listened.

"After that last little blunder of the double booking I really wanted to show you how adept I really am at sorting…." he paused, searching for the right word. It never came. "Things. So I don't want you to be put out of your business routine in any way. This funeral was requested for twelve o'clock but I insisted it be at ten o'clock instead to give us all plenty of time for the two o'clock wedding, eh? Now don't you think that was a grand idea?"

Father O'Rourke gave me a huge, boyish grin. He really thought I would be delighted with the final outcome but all I could see was that coffin casting a morbid shadow on all his optimistic sunshine. I would be flitting about the church trying to ignore, but ultimately working around, a dead body just a few feet away. It was too weird, but it got even worse. Our conversation was very one-sided as I still could not express my horror and the priest took the floor, unperturbed.

"So I'll be in my study with that beer, the one that USED to be cold, if you need me," He laughed at his wit. "Just come straight through when you finish and I can lock up." He turned to leave towards the big, now intimidating, oak door. It somehow looked even bigger, heavier and sounded more groaning than when I came in a few moments ago. He was deserting me!

"Father," I implored, "You're not seriously going to leave me here alone with a dead person, a

118

corpse. I can't work like this, under these circumstances. I would be scared stiff!" Scared to death, scared stiff – every word conjured up corpses and coffins.

"I'll just have to come back tomorrow after the funeral." This was a hollow threat for I - nor any of my team - would have no time whatsoever to return to the church before Lorna Bond's wedding here tomorrow. There were still oodles of other deliveries to do then. It was now or never. But I wasn't letting the Father off the hook by sharing that confession.

"Couldn't you have postponed this funeral till Monday? Why did it have to be tomorrow? Really!" I threw at him crossly.

He had a tiny twinkle in his eye as he ghoulishly shot back, "What? Two more days in this heat? It wouldn't be pretty, not pretty at all! I've seen you in motion, dealing with life's slings and arrows in a fine, strong way. You're a much better woman than this. Now get on with your work and don't be silly." He was absolutely enjoying my discomfort. "And don't be afraid of poor Thomas lying there in his coffin. Oh, he was a bit of a wild man when he was alive, indeed he was! But not now. Sure, you'll never meet a more harmless soul in all your life, than him!"

It infuriated me to think he was absolutely right. I knew I was freaking out unnecessarily but just the idea of a dead person lying nearby as I worked away alone made me shiver. Alone. That was the killer. I strained to remember the path of the maze we had used to come in from the house, in case I needed a quick escape. I really began to wish I had dropped that trail of crumbs – but at least the big oak door was there. I tried it as soon as the priest left, making sure it wasn't locked.

"Pull yourself together," I spoke out loud to myself for reassurance. "You're being stupid and ridiculous. What? Are you expecting the corpse to suddenly jump up and shout 'Boo!' You must be nuts." I glanced over to the coffin again to make sure nothing was going on, just in case. I gradually, eventually, moved back into big girl mode and focused on the flowers, the job in hand. Less than an hour later I was driving home. I have never decorated a church so quickly. Ever....

In Scotland it is generally considered a dream to have a run of hot sunny weather, but when that actually transpires it seems many people just can't handle it. All the shops run out of ice cream, ice lollies, lettuce, tomatoes and salad cream. Add to this our seriously overcrowded parks and beaches, and the 'gorgeous warm spell' gets to be a bloody nuisance. At least it does for wedding planners.

If Lorna Bond had been praying for good weather for her big day then bingo! However, this particular Saturday in September was just too good and should have been dealt with differently, on reflection. In any situation and particularly at weddings, when it rains we run for cover, dive to shelter under awnings and trees as if the drops were poison. But when a heinous heat hurls itself upon us, we just stand and smile, convinced it's heaven sent and determine to enjoy it, no matter what. We don't think of sunshine and suffering in the same sentence, but suffer is what poor Lorna did on her wedding day, in droves.

I headed up to St. Paul's which had been cleared of the previous evening's sombre coffins and hearses, leaving plenty of space for our wedding frippery. Mourning would be replaced with merriment as guests arrived at the church nice and early, the ladies confident that their new chiffon dresses and expensive hats would have an opportunity to be paraded in the sunshine.

I had organized most of this affair and now I was driving one of the limos while keeping an eye on the smooth flow of the proceedings. Chauffeuring, if I had the chance, was one way of doing this discreetly. My stalwart driver companions, Archie and Ben busied themselves sorting out coolers in the boots of the limos while the ceremony was taking place. On freezing winter wedding days it was flasks of hot chocolate, for we aimed to comfort. Today it would be ice cold cokes, lemonade, bottled water and for the bridal couple only – a nice, crisp bottle of champagne. All of this would be appreciated today, but the champagne was mainly for the benefit of the photo shoot at a nearby beauty spot. There would be no popping of corks outside the church – ever. Protocol forbade it so it was saved for the park.

"I'm not what you would call a drinker," said Archie, wiping his forehead with a clean hankie. His chauffeur cap and the oppressive heat had caused him to sweat. "But if there was a cold lager there, I could just murder it."

"But not when I'm driving, of course," he added, looking at me sheepishly.

"Have some water, lads. That'll keep us going today. All the fancies are for our clients. As well you know, Archie." This was a pointless jab since Archie never touched booze, driving or not.

"It'll be torture hanging around in this heat for photos," Ben tugged at his tie as if he was choking. "When I think of the times we've complained about the winter weddings and the cold conditions. I'm not sure I wouldn't swap this stinger for a frosty day."

"I don't think I know the photo guy for this affair," Archie cut in. "Who is he, anyway?"

We both glanced over to the young cameraman busy fidgeting with his photographic equipment at the other side of the church car park. I told him the photographer was a workmate of the bridal couple who were both police officers. Since Lorna had assigned us to do practically all of her big day except for this one service I had been curious about him and his work, too.

After she had chosen to eliminate our photo service from the Package, Lorna assured me her replacement friend would do a fine job. "Harry works with us at Police Headquarters in Glasgow and we've seen some of his beautiful wedding pictures. It's his weekend hobby. I'm sure he'll be excellent and he's very keen," she assured me.

Since he wasn't part of my own team I had contacted the photographer a few weeks prior to the big day to make sure we would all be on the same page with work schedule and locations. I was curious about his wedding experience too and asked him about it.

"Well, I've only done a couple of weddings but I am an experienced photographer. That's what I do for a living, after all." He sounded a bit hesitant when I pushed him further. "I take pictures all the time."

"What kind of pictures?" I asked innocently.

"Well….I photograph the dead bodies in the mortuary….!"

I am not prone to being dumbstruck but that last piece of info did the trick. I hung up quickly, mumbling thanks and reassuring myself silently that as long as the wedding party didn't actually move or breathe, all would be fine and normal. At least normal for Harry.

The bride was a straightforward client. She had given us carte blanche control over her wedding plans, her dress fittings were uncomplicated to be involved in and she was appreciative of the little personal touches that came with our service. Lorna was tall and svelte with a sense of style, illustrated by this special day when she had her long fair hair tucked into a twist at the back, helping to hold the garland of fresh flowers we had created for her. Her dress was fairytale, an off the shoulder lightly beaded satin ballgown style – not white, but a subtle shade of pale silver grey. I hoped for the umpteenth time that Harry would do a good job with the pictures. I definitely wanted a large portrait of this stunning bride in the salon.

The crew had the drinks safely tucked in ice coolers and we tried to stay cool ourselves while the ceremony took place, imagining we were in tank tops and shorts, not in business suits. As everyone reappeared after the service, Harry took the usual church steps pictures. I noticed people in the lineup scowling against the sun but fortunately that section took only ten or fifteen minutes. Then the group progressed away from the steps towards an island of tallish conifers in the church garden where they continued to deal with the same uncomfortable mid-afternoon heat. It must have been awkward to keep smiling with full sun in the face but Lorna and her groom Sean seemed to be managing it well. I noticed the bride frown and wobble a bit towards the end of the half hour session, and so I checked the time. Yes, our schedule was about to be blown. I had a word with Harry reminding him it was time to leave the church grounds and get to our next photo location. At least he could creatively snap away there while the champagne was being popped and cold sodas handed out.

There was a small pond and park near the church and we were familiar with it. Lots of tall bushes and trees were set back from the water which offered half sun and half shade. It would have been perfect but the man with the camera had other ideas, so everyone was exposed to full glare again as they lined up at the water's edge where Harry wanted to make a feature of the backdrop of the pond. The whole party was melting like ice cream as we pulled out the drinks from the coolers. The bridal couple stuck to the champagne and did not so much sip it, as guzzle it from the flutes whilst Harry recorded the moment. The bubbly seemed to pick the couple up a little which was just as well, for there were plenty more photos to come.

Forty minutes at the pond park and we were still going strong. Forty-five minutes was the maximum allotted time but I had noticed Lorna looking anxious in her discomfort and it puzzled me why Harry had not caught onto this. I checked with him about the time but he was adamant that he needed more pictures. Just as I was reminding him again about the schedule, I noticed Lorna sway. Enough was enough. Harry begged for more time and I explained he had already abused the agreed total timetable for this wedding, plus he still had an opportunity to take more at the reception. Then I emphasized my main concern to him.

"Everyone is heat exhausted, particularly the bride. Look…."

As I turned towards the bride, hoping to make him aware of her situation, poor Lorna teetered again. She looked as if…

Yes, she did. She fainted right there on the cool green grass.

I knew I should have put my foot down sooner. I mused that if it was this guy's job to take pictures of dead people then he was definitely on the right road to increasing his clientele. I reckoned another five minutes and half of the wedding party would have expired.

Lots of cold water and much fussing later saw Lorna reviving. Everyone, including our crematory cameraman Harry got the message that it was time to head to the hotel and cool shelter. Once the party was dropped off at the reception I did my rounds, checking centerpieces, cake and so on, before leaving. But first I had to make sure our beautiful bride was surviving. It was cheering to note she had a champagne glass in her hand as she greeted guests but I could sense her queasiness, confirmed by her chief bridesmaid who whispered that Lorna had, just a few minutes before, been sick in the ladies' room. Classic heat exhaustion. I left hoping fervently that she would get over it.

I wish I could go on to report that we had a happy ending to this story, but not to be. Minutes after sitting down at the top table, poor Lorna passed out again and had to retire to bed in the bridal suite, attended in turns by her mother, the groom, and the groom's mum. The rest of the main table all had to play host while poor Lorna missed the reception meal, the cake-cutting, the speeches, the dancing.

To summarize….she missed her own wedding. Heat stroke had done her in. Sunshine and an over-zealous photographer.

To Hire or Not to Hire

When does a customer become a client? When my bridal business started I was hiring out gowns and catering to a specific market of mainly working-class customers. I only had customers then, but as spending habits and units of sale grew with an expanding business, they became clients. Since my relationship with them spanned a couple of years on average, then the transition to client is understandable. But there is more to it than the obvious turn of phrase.

Truly, my brand-new wedding hire business in 1971 was uncomplicated. Life seemed much simpler. Expectations were more low-key. Weddings themselves – or at least the ones I managed - were conducted without aspiration to be anything other than the union of a couple, a family celebration of a new beginning and the establishment of a fresh branch of the family tree.

The majority of weddings coming my way were not planned years before the date, as they became latterly. Families were not required to accumulate thousands of pounds for designer gowns, fancy hotels and upgraded services.

The average wedding at that time would have been at a local venue, probably with no ambitious location photography other than the use of church grounds. Later at the village or cooperative hall or community centre reception, the photographing of the cake-cutting ceremony would generally signal the end of formal proceedings and the party would begin.

Throughout the 70's the nature of the business evolved primarily through social changes. Over the period of our forty years of existence all predilections, expectations and protocol, based mainly on changing sexual attitudes, determined our direction. And the contrast in those attitudes over that period was extremely dramatic. Hardly a month went by in the salad days of the company, when I did not cater to a young girl who was being rushed to the marriage table by her parents due to a pregnancy. Lack of previous planning in such a situation would demand economic adjustment – so hiring a wedding gown readily and fairly cheaply was an answer for most families.

Half of the time I would have been forewarned of the prevailing circumstances by the customer herself, or more likely by her mother, but just as often I was not brought into the loop. So instead, I honed my instincts to gauge a situation and would tread delicately around it. The main issue for me was the size of bridal dress required and very often the uncertainty around that question spoke volumes about the hush-hush situation.

"Oh, I'm a size 12 just now," the bride would inform me, quietly blushing. "But I'm sure I'll need about a size 14 in three months' time, on the wedding day." Sometimes this was the only clue to what was going on. I knew how to handle it. Just don't talk about it.

Occasionally I was tripped up. Believe it or not, some girls would let me bash on regardless with a 'current size' knowing full well the dress would almost certainly not fit in a few months' time. But if I suspected that there was something afoot, I spoke up. Someone had to. "Is there anything you would like to share with me regarding the size of the dress? Remember, we're all girls together." Most times this cracked the ice but I had to be pretty sure that my hunch was correct or it would have been embarrassing. Interestingly, I often heard a great sigh of relief at this point, which is understandable.

This all sounds so crazy now, but it was an amazingly real predicament at the time. The very idea of being married at all with all the frills and flounces was particularly ludicrous when girls chose to wobble down the aisle in the advanced stages of pregnancy, sometimes with only two or three months before their due date. With the propriety being that marriage should come before babies, it was a given that the couple would tie knots beforehand, ridiculous looking or not. I know none of my brides actually gave birth right there in the church but as I look back I sometimes wonder how we all escaped the event.

These early days brought me probably my youngest bride ever. I had not been in business very long and she showed up with her mother who herself was only thirty-three years old. The future bride was expecting a baby and her mother, far from disapproving, was excited and happy for her sixteen year-old. The conversation was open and frank and I learned that she herself had been married in the same circumstances at the same age, which I had already surmised. She had had a good marriage to a good man and she was obviously confident her daughter would follow suit. I have often wondered if she did. This is not an unusual thought process for me as you can imagine. Over the years I've harked back to the weddings of these days - the simpler days - and recalled my involvement in making them possible, of being instrumental in their happy, if uncertain, beginnings. But what about the endings - were they happy too?

Colour choices for wedding dresses at this time were white, white and…white! Snow white, even. Virginal white. And that was a great problem for many. Believe you me, I was more than a little relieved when the ivory wedding dress emerged – salvation! Of course there was still a certain stigma attached to this and unlike nowadays, brides were not likely to choose ivory as a gown colour simply because it suited their skin tone. Oh, no. Ivory was mostly a red flag to the gossip-mongers that our bride had already been to the rodeo, so to speak. She was a soiled, wanton whatever….I suppose a pregnant bride just could not win. If she sported white, then she was going against the mores of propriety. If she chose ivory, then she flew the flag of the floozy. All of this sounds archaic, I know. Attitudes have changed so much that we do not even recognize them as attitudes. So anything goes. And over the years in our salon we sold almost every colour of wedding dress to our independent liberated female clients - black and red being particular favourites.

Hiring was the primary function of the wedding company launched in 1971. Forty years later this service was still a popular one and the salon benefitted from being able to offer brides the choice of sale or hire, which not all bridal shops do. Hiring had so many advantages – it was cheaper and a bride would not be left with an expensive cleaning bill afterwards, let alone the challenge of finding a large area in a small fitted wardrobe for storage. But hiring was not always suitable for everyone – not even for those women who swore it was the best practical option ever. There was a time to hire, and for an incurable romantic – a time to buy….

We should have known from the outset that Norma Burns was not a strong candidate for hiring. The truth of it was her choice of dress was amazingly expensive and she did have a budget – not a tiny one, but not a free rein one, either. On her first sojourn into the salon to check us out she fell in love with a bouffant, ivory silk puffball of a dress that shouted Princess Di.

Dresses like this, in the aftermath of the royal wedding, were extremely popular and our rails held many copycat versions of the core dress available for either rent or sale. They were not cheap, mainly because of the vast quantity of pure silk required to create such a gown. To hire, albeit an expensive hire, was the much more pragmatic option and we found ourselves busy dealing with both sides of the market.

Yes, it was sartorial love at first sight for Norma. Throughout our client/planner relationship I heard her goo-goo more about THAT dress, disturbingly more than she ever did about her supposedly true love – the groom. But perhaps this wasn't just exclusive to her, when I think long and hard about such things.

The catalyst for hiring versus purchasing was, apart from being cheaper, usually 'why not just hire – when am I likely to wear it again, really?' I do not recall exactly but I'm sure Norma would have uttered these words.

However, if I had had a crystal ball just then I would have told Norma: "Many, many times."

Norma's wedding was a delight for her and she was far from being a nervous bride. Every moment was a joy but the trouble was, she just didn't want it to end, even months after the fact. She was a fairly tall, suicide blonde with Sophia Loren exotic green eyes. Being a striking, very glamourous girl, she regularly modelled at fashion shows throughout the county, most of them related to charity benefits and the like. For the finale of these shows she would help to market our salon by donning THE dress with full accessories, all provided by us, and impressing the audience. The marketing aspect for us was absolutely unimportant to her. She merely relished the opportunity to don THE dress again and parade in it.

Another post-wedding habit Norma acquired was keeping in touch by popping into the salon at least every three weeks or so. I strongly suspected that perhaps this was not so much to enjoy our society as it was to revisit her beautiful ex-wedding gown. Even if there was no fashion show excuse, she would still manage access. We just got on with our work and merely pointed to the rail where her dress lived.

"Oh! Here it is! Oh, my God, it is still absolutely gorgeous. I get all shivery just looking at it! Do you know I still have dreams about my big day - and if I could I would do it all again – over and over! Mostly just to wear that dress."

This became such a regular occurrence that we would occasionally allow her to try it on in the shop for the thrill of it. Of course, this was green-lighted only after she had removed her rather heavy make-up – Norma was always fully made-up and glamourized. So there were many occasions when she managed to maintain her relationship with the gown.

"I really should have bought this dress, not hired it. I just want to live in it, honestly!"

Obviously she was right. Some girls bought dresses from us and after the wedding stuffed the creation into the back of the wardrobe without any thought. Deed done, now let's get on with the rest of our lives. Then there was Norma, the romantic dreamer who constantly paid homage.

Strange as it sounds, the fashion shows became a bit of a problem for the salon since Norma was establishing herself as a one-trick pony.

After two or three different shows with the same girl in the same dress, I had to spell out the problem.

"You always want to wear YOUR dress so some of the audience just might think we have no others. Choose another next time and you'll still be beautiful. We don't want to overplay our hand now, do we?"

She agreed, but reluctantly. We were still taking orders for sales and hires of her dress, basically a sample, but we wanted to vary the offerings at shows. They say there is no such thing as bad publicity, but how about the monotonous kind?

Towards the end of the season I had good news for Norma when she exercised one of her dress-visitation rights. "We'll be selling off the samples soon so you could buy the dress then. We'll make sure you get it and put it aside for you."

She was ecstatic and rightly so, for it meant she could play bride every single day of her life. Forget peeling the potatoes or mopping the floors – why be dull? She could play Cinderella instead. The girl was a one-off....

Before the transaction ever took place I was contacted by the producer of a Scottish Television programme. They were having a live discussion the following week, with an audience. The subject was weddings, the point being 'Are They Worth the Expense?"

The producer asked if I would be willing, as a wedding expert, to appear on the show in front of a live audience. My role would be to justify from my own perspective, the excess. The show would discuss all the services - limousines, photos, cakes, invites, flowers, videos and of course, dresses. Since we supplied all of these services I felt confident speaking on any facet of wedding preparation. In fact, I thought I could really offer a complete and different angle to the subject matter.

"I'm sure I can come up with some interesting material for your programme. In fact I could try to produce a former client who would be qualified to provide her opinion. As a bonus, maybe I could arrange to have that person in full wedding gear, too." I had rather recklessly volunteered this plan with Norma in mind. However, I knew I would not have to persuade her. This would be the extra icing on top of the icing of her preserved top tier of wedding cake. (To explain… the top tier would often be stored for a first baby's christening)

On the night of the programme, I discovered that most of the invited television audience was against the frivolity of weddings. Where had they found these people? Nonetheless they were the majority and had plenty to say on the stupidity of lashing out a few coppers on one big day. What about the mortgage? Mortgage? Some of the bah-humbuggers put forward that you would be lucky to get a mortgage since you had spent every penny of a house deposit on the W word. People got themselves into debt unnecessarily and there was too much stress associated with the W word. It just went on and on. Even the bill for dry-cleaning gowns post W came under scrutiny by the scrooges dotted around the studio. We went back and forth and being in the minority, I was relieved I had brought my sister with me for moral support as I faced the madding crowd.

I argued my own points but of course by any standards I was seen to have an axe to grind. I felt it was time. Yes, it was time to produce my trump card, my ace in-the-hole.

 Enter Norma, who had been waiting in the wings to make her cue, fully clad in her most favourite of favourite outfits bar none.

I stood proudly and faced the enemy, adopting my best Ally McBeal posture. "Norma was my client for her wedding several months ago. She had a beautiful, opulent affair on her big day, all managed by my company and she does not grudge a bit of the outgoings on her wedding. She will now tell you why…."

Norma took over willingly and paraded herself in all her beloved finery to the dreamkillers, the doubting Thomases, the sceptics. She spoke convincingly and clearly from her heart, not having to recite any phony lines. She delivered romantic, idealistic words as she beamed her way round the studio stage, showing off her dress and finally revelling over the conversion of some cynics. The fact was that she had impressed the crowd and there was plenty of envious eyeballing going around. Not one of them could have argued against her convincing stance on weddings and their validity in modern life. Yes, she may have looked like a pretty, luscious meringue gliding up and down that stage, but come on – who doesn't have a fancy for meringues on occasion? She glowed the way a bride SHOULD glow, happy and delighted to share her happiness with everyone.

As my wedding career progressed over the decades even I had to admit that sometimes there was too much focus on the frippery and extravagance of the wedding, and possibly not enough on the future marriage. But I do still feel that going the extra mile is important. A couple should be overjoyed to share their commitment with close friends and family and naturally there should be some expense. So long as plans are not totally over the top, then it's worth it. That's because weddings ARE a big deal and for a couple, this represents the beginning of the rest of their lives together, hopefully.

Forgetting practicalities, Norma was certainly one bride who should have bought, not hired her dress. But she was a one-off. I can think of no one else who reacted to the whole wedding fairytale quite like her. I often wondered if she actually did, after we finally donated the dress to her, try it on every single day, including Christmas and Bank Holidays. Nothing would surprise me. It is a glorious image – her mopping the floors and peeling the potatoes with it on, fully made up and her tiara sparkling under the bright kitchen lights. How delightful.

Bouquet of Thorned Roses

A big, fat wedding was paramount for Maggie Frome.   Most brides enjoy the fuss, but some do crave more frills than others. I have experienced brides who took the simplest dress, the tiniest bouquet and set off happily to the registry office for a quickee half hour ceremony. Not our Maggie. She started celebrating the minute she set the date and for her it was Lottery-winning, Oscar-achieving stuff.

Miss Frome was a gem of a girl. To use a good honest Scottish phrase, 'she was a nice lassie'. I felt she was a special person straightaway at our first meeting and my hunch was truly confirmed over the next ten months as I trotted along beside her up the preparatory bridal path.

Maggie booked our deluxe package less than a year before the big day, which was to be the

143

following May. This is not a long time for planning the myriad of services vital to a successful big day and most of our wedding couples chose to book WA-AY ahead of the date, but I'm not sure she could have endured the tension of waiting a long time. I believe that for her it was already a hundred years away and the time could not have gone fast enough. She wanted it to be the following week.

"I know I'm not being cool about all this, but I don't care," she told us at the first meeting. "I dream about it every night and think about it constantly the rest of the time. I'm in limbo. Oh, and I've bought every wedding magazine there is – imagine!"

Yes, every staff member could imagine. For when Maggie came into see us there was a giant buzz - so much so that even other clients who happened to be there were caught up in the Maggie magic. She was infectious in a super, sweet way. A customer said one time after she went home, "She seems to spread fairy dust, what a lovely personality…I feel like inviting her to MY wedding so everyone would be sure to have a good time."

Her OTT charisma cheerily overflowed into her wedding choices. The dress, for example. It was absolutely not tailored or simple or any of these sophisticated things. It was full and layered with frills and sequins and extremely fussy. Truly, it was a big fat candy floss…and just what Maggie loved. She was keen for everyone to know she was keen and we knew they had just better notice as she marched down that aisle. Her white veil was long and firmly framed the extended train of her glittering gown, which was trimmed with picot edging and little jeweled starbursts. The whole thing spelled ultimate bride as we helped to pile on the gaudy glaze, all the way up to the top of her head, which would sport the penultimate set of dazzling crystal side combs. Razzle dazzle time, indeed.

Maggie's hair was thick and long, probably her star feature. There were glints of copper through her light brown tresses and they kind of twinkled too as she stood on the shop dais, the sun from the window catching her crowning glory. She was about five feet five, a reasonable height and had fine white Irish skin. Her radiance and natural prettiness made you overlook the fact that she was inclined to plumpness, but she carried it well and it was not mentioned by her at all. We were so used to girls promising us and themselves that they would drop a size and join a slimmers' club and just eat cottage cheese. Usually though, these were the girls who were already a size ten or twelve, hardly gargantuan. We all had a feeling Maggie was comfortable in her own Celtic skin which is what matters. I think her motto was, 'hey, if life throws you a size 18 dress, buy a bigger bra....'

As she stood on the dais wearing her choice and absorbing a long look at herself in our big mirror she cried tears of joy. And that's what our boxes and boxes of tissues were for.

"I just love it all. God, it's my dream come true," she sniffed, blowing her nose on the hankie I had just handed her. Yes, listening and Kleenex were vital components to the smoothness of our operation. "When Hugh said we could get married I couldn't believe it. I mean, we've been living together for four years, so it's about time."

"Did he get down on one knee and propose?" asked Jinty, our ever-so-romantic assistant. I had a tissue ready for her, too.

I thought Maggie was about to fall off her little bridal stage laughing. "No. He absolutely did not. He never asked me. I was the one who suggested it." She blew her elegant chiseled nose again and smiled.

"Remember, I said 'suggested' – not asked! I had a feeling we would still be in the same situation six more years down the line – and with three or four kids in tow – if I hadn't!"

Marlon threw in, "Oh, yeah! As in I SUGGEST you take out the rubbish, dear, or I SUGGEST you fetch me a glass of wine!"

Everyone cheered on the bride's honesty and there was a ton of good feeling circulating around. Except for Maggie's mum. I noticed she was forcing smiles. Perhaps she was shy, unlike her daughter, but she sat on our gold-velvet covered sofa and observed. Just observed. Was she angry with her lovely daughter, or perhaps the groom? Mothers didn't always necessarily approve of modern trends, especially involving this 'proposal' of marriage. Was that it? I knew that she had two sons still living at home, Maggie being the only girl. Perhaps that had something to do with it, too. She did not want to let her only girl go, or maybe she just didn't want her to go to this particular fellow. Our salon could generate a pleasant confidante atmosphere for clients, especially clients like the open bookish Maggie. We were a bit like a hairdresser's shop or psychologists couch where many of the clients told you EVERYTHING. Maggie fitted into that category, certainly - but she had not offered up info on her mother and her approval, or otherwise, of the wedding. Or Mum's attitude to the groom.

And somehow we were not au fait with asking. It was a wee cloud we brushed aside, for we wanted nothing but sunshine for this girl, but we were soon to find out why this slightly sad mum appeared to be under the weather.

Early into the initial stages of planning, the groom's party came in for fittings for their kilt outfits. Since this was not my department, I was focusing on other business when Marlon, our only male member of staff filled me in on the progress, or lack of it.

"Call me a tittle tattle or whatever you want," he stage-whispered and commanded my attention with his right hand which was flaying about like Shirley Bassey in Concert. The other hand was firmly planted on his left hip, "but that Hughie, the groom one, he'll need a flipping shotgun at his back at that wedding, mark my words."

What? I had been so immersed in my own work that I had lost track of Marlon's particular booking. Which wedding? Who was this Hughie? Marlon filled me in on the details and my heart started to crack, just a little. Oh, God, this was Maggie's fiancé and suddenly the proposal story in the salon some weeks before came rushing back to me. I probed Marlon further and of course, he willingly obliged.

"He's bitched and moaned all the way through the fitting. He keeps on about the clothes but it's obvious he's mad about something else – like getting married! He says the kilt is too tight, the jacket sleeves aren't right and that he wants a bigger sporran." At this, Marlon rolled his eyes. "I just said, 'Babe, we all want bigger sporrans, but life isn't like that, so just get used to it!' Not a smile, not a chuckle…"

At this, he minced off back to the fitting rooms wearing his blue plastic tape measure round his neck as if it were a fresh and fragrant Hawaiin lei. God, he had style, that Marlon. On anyone else the tatty tape would have looked like an old broken luggage strap.

I watched closely, from this point on, to get a feel of that kilt fitting. Everyone else but Hughie seemed to be ok. Marlon was spot on for it seemed this groom just did not want to be there. When it finally wrapped up, the party agreed to go off to the pub together, not an original thought when it came to men's fittings, I have to say. I introduced myself to the gloomy groom as he was leaving and I was not offended when he appeared very unexcited to meet me. I cared not a jot for him - but his lovely bride's face just happened to haunt me. Yep, we had a super keen bride and an extremely reluctant groom.

Oh, Maggie! Well, they say opposites attract and personality-wise these two were polar opposites. What a misery-guts! Perhaps he thought himself superior, worthy of a more glamourous female, but to my mind she would have had to be myopic – totally short-sighted, for Hugh was no Brad Pitt. He had mousey thinning hair and was of similar height to his bride - not tall for a man. He was also not svelte – probably a good thing for a kilt wearer since sturdy fellows carry the kilt outfit better, but even here he definitely had too much of a belly. Perhaps he realized this at the fitting and it irked him…

Marlon looked ready to collapse. He plopped his slender, almost six foot frame on the velvet sofa and appealed to anyone who was listening, "Please put the kettle on 'cos my poor head is splitting. No, no chocolate biscuits, just aspirin. I want to lose five pounds by the end of the month. Angelo is taking me away for a well-deserved luxury weekend at Loch Lomond." He turned to me as an afterthought. "Don't worry, I'm not leaving till all the kilts go out on that weekend. Cripes, I could do with a wee fling after that vile scenario in there. Love match? Love? No way!"

He was prompted to start singing 'What's Love Got to do With It' in the wrong key, so we all got out of the way very quickly to focus on the tea.

A month before Maggie's big day we did final fittings for her gowns. We always HOPED these fittings would be final, even if experience had taught us to expect the unexpected. Fortunately everything was fairly straightforward and in fact the brilliant girl herself had lost seven pounds which made her wedding dress sit beautifully, not taut as it had been originally, but skimming over her curves softly and flattering her whole figure. It was always surprising to me that a hearty seven pound loss would not necessarily mean a dress size decrease. Instead it would simply make the same size SIT better. Still fitted, but not tight. Whatever, Maggie was over the moon.

"It was easy for me to lose 'cos I've been too nervous to eat much and too busy to bother."

I asked her about her intended and if he cooked dinner occasionally. Perhaps I was getting nosey but I just had to know a bit more about the groom.

"You kidding? These days – well any days – he's down the pub so he gets fed there. Suits me." She shrugged then turned to gaze one more time in the mirror. "Look at this! Can't wait now…"

Maggie's mum was restrained, there was definitely something still bugging her. But this time around, having met the not-so-charming fiancé, I had a good idea what it was. On their way out of the shop she thanked me politely for the work we had done. "You've made my daughter so happy and it shows. I know you'll make it a special day for her." Yes, she seemed to be happy for her Maggie but I still wondered how she truly felt about the marriage.

Now it was time for the guys' final fittings and again our man Marlon took control.

"I took extra vitamin B12 this morning to hold me over," he shared with the staff. "I know I have the patience of Job but there are limits when it comes to this thug of a groomie...."

I stood by just in case there were any incidents and sure enough the groom was totally predictable. For a time everything seemed to be going well, then I heard Hugh yell at Marlon, "Why could you no' have got it right the first time. I telt ye it would be tight, I telt ye."

After a barrage of abuse, Marlon dived into our little kitchen for respite and I followed him in. I knew he would be looking to take an extra breath and wash it down with diet cola, but if he needed help I was willing to straighten Hughie out. Normally Marlon had our male clients, whom I suspected were normally a little terrified of him, in the palm of his Palmolive-soft hands, but this was slightly uncharted territory.

152

"That Shuggie is a bitch. Imagine blaming me for his kilt being too tight when he already told me straight out he was down the pub every night gobbling pub grub and drinking beer. I told him beer and chips were full of calories and fattening but he doesn't like the truth." He strode over, fuming, to the open door of the kitchen, then as if to appease himself, started glancing prissily at his toned frame in the salon mirror several feet away.

"God, when I think of what I've sacrificed to look like this," and he stood back for my inspection, arms outstretched to display his sleek lithe lines. "I tell you, you don't get to look like this by being at the boozer every night and putting pints away. No, most nights of the working week I subsist on a Lean Cuisine and an orange."

"Ah, you look great, Marlon. But then, you've been on that new 'F' Plan Diet," I put in, trying to be supportive to his vanity. Marlon's diets were always a topic for discussion in the salon.

"I was, I was, but it was so disappointing. It turned out the 'F' stood for fibre, come on! I thought it would be something much more interesting. Boring, boring…" He sighed deeply and took a long cool gulp of water. "It's like bloody Braveheart out there, but I'm ready for the fray!"

Revived, he returned to the highlandwear battlefield again and I wished him luck.

Flowers happened to be one of our most profitable services and I constantly tried to increase the volume of a flower wedding order. As well as the obvious bouquets, church and table flowers we offered presentation bouquets or baskets for the couple's mothers, a nice touch to acknowledge parental support and usually these were presented publicly after the wedding speeches. Never one to shy away from increasing a unit of sale even more, I would also ask a groom if he wished us to deliver a bouquet of red roses to his loved one as a personal touch between them, on the morning of the wedding. This was rarely refused, men always being grateful for help to keep them on the right track romantically. They would usually pay there and then and sign with a loving message, the little card that we would include in the delivery. Yes, grooms usually aimed to please, but not this particular one.

Before Hugh left the shop on that final fitting I asked him – tentatively – if he would like us to provide this type of service. I should have known what his reaction would be.

"Flowers? More flowers! Have we not spent enough money on all this hilarity already! I'll be sending no flowers, so forget it!"

I took this as a refusal and closed the order book. He stormed out angrily and I was grateful the only other people in the shop at the time had been his own party. Of course I got it in the ear from Marlon.

"Did you really think that yon a-hole was going to convert to being a nice chap and send his precious bride fresh flowers? Come on!"

Of course he was absolutely right. Why did I even think of asking him to treat his good lady on her magical day. Poor Maggie. I felt like sending her flowers myself. God knows she would need them.

The run up to Maggie's day was mad, happy chaos. She was in and out of the shop getting her dresses, then back for the accessories to accommodate hairdresser trials and then once more to hand in chocolates to our staff. Like we needed chocolates. It was giggles galore that day as she fake-modelled her new coiffure because her hairdresser had caused her to have a bad hair day for the hair trial.

"Look at this, it's supposed to be a chignon and it looks more like an old toilet brush," she burst out and we all collapsed into fits of laughter. "But I'm going back there again later for another go. In the name of the wee man, think positive thoughts for me, please!"

Everything else was in place that sunny, warm Saturday when I started to tick the last box – the flowers for Durwall Church. Another member of the team and I had taken along buckets of beautiful roses and lilies in preparation for arranging. We knew what was called for and almost exactly how long we would be to set up three large arrangements around the dais and one in the church foyer. The pew ends were made up and ready to be attached before we left the workshop. I knew that the church would be complete at least half an hour before the groom and best man's arrival and a full hour before the wedding itself. Even early arrival guests were unlikely to show up more than a half hour before the ceremony which was important for my company. It was bad form to be seen there still working at the last minute in front of guests. There were other weddings that day besides Maggie's so we had been busy and this church job was the last on the list.

Unfortunately this was the church of the dreaded Rev Warren, a minister who gave those who had the audacity to enter his church on business, particularly wedding business, a very rough ride. I stupidly had not allowed extra time for his fussing and placement demands when he hovered around annoyingly, asking why THAT had to be there, could it be over HERE – in other words, the usual stuff he always pulled. I told him I had my instructions from my client and was answerable to her alone. He must have sensed I was in no mood because he backed off rather meekly. The last bloom was placed and I let my assistant Bet go on home, planning to tidy and clear up the job myself, then head home for sustenance.

Of course, I should have known. The minister had found another scapegoat. Jay, the videographer contracted by me to cover Maggie's wedding, had just arrived. I looked nervously at my watch before remembering he had been determined to be early in order to check out the layout for his camera positions, since this was his first time in Durwall. For that reason, I believe the Rev possibly thought he was an independent, not part of my team. Naturally, he started to lay down the law to poor Jay who although youngish and respectful, was also highly experienced and a creative videographer.

157

Jay was subjected to the same, 'special placement' treatment. He was not to block that corner there, or to position in this part over here and actually it would be far better, according to the Rev, if he could stay well away from the communion table and move to the entry door of the church to take the footage from way back there, about one hundred yards away. Fine for him. The video, however would be ghastly.

Rev Warren was obviously determined to triumph at one power struggle since he hadn't succeeded with me, and I stayed silent for a short while as I finished picking up leaves and clearing up my tools, hoping Jay would stand up to him and his demands. But it was awkward for the young man – he possibly felt he could not be over arrogant with the vicar in my presence, not confident that he would have my blessing, so I stepped into the one-sided feud. Quicker than it took to say 'amen' I cut into his barrage of grievances.

I reminded him that this was a very special day for my client, who simply wanted a clear, memorable video of her wedding and in order to do that Jay would have to set up professionally.

"Of course, he will compromise a little, but you must work with him so that everyone is happy. Isn't that the right thing to do here?"

The vicar looked taken aback. It was clear he hadn't known Jay and I were on the same team. He yielded somewhat.

"Yes, of course the bride can have her wish, but I do not want the video man lurking around this area here," as he spread out his gangly arms vaguely in the direction of the communion table. "We will all be tripping over him. I do not see why he cannot be at the back of the church, not the front."

"You and I both know, sir, that his placement at the back of the church would be a complete waste of time. It would be much too far back to achieve clarity in the film."

This was infuriating. Warren and his ruddy power struggles. My mouth had not yet begun to foam but I was sure it was just a matter of time because there was a lot at stake here, I had a lot to protect. It upset me to think of Maggie and her dream of a fantastic wedding. I had to defend her right to have it sealed for all time on this video. I hadn't had lunch yet and I guess I decided to choose Rev Warren as my dish of the day. I could be sent to hell for all eternity, but what the....

"No, I have to insist on this," I almost yelled across the dais. Time was rolling on and I was still trying to tidy up my mess and tools from my work with the fresh church flowers. I began to wish I had held on to Bet instead of letting her nip off home. The baptismal font nearby seemed to be beckoning to me. Beckoning me to keep calm and remember where I was. It had beautiful carvings with saintly proverbs, words of goodness and love to inspire us to live better lives. But I felt that right at that moment the Rev Warren was not at all displaying any goodness, love or even basic empathy for his fellow man. He was being officious in the extreme, and I told him so.

"I think you forget that the church members are entitled to some say and you're giving no thought to their needs, particularly to today's bride."

All this time Jay stood by silently, poker-faced, watching and listening intently. At one point I was sure he would sit in one of the gleaming polished pews and take out a bag of popcorn. I don't think he had seen this movie before, although sad to say I had, since it was not the first time the vicar and I had crossed swords. Rev Warren's mouth was wide open and seemed to be stuck in that position. The thought occurred to me that he might have had a stroke, but no, he found his voice again, albeit a slightly softer, weaker voice than before.

The heated confab continued for another five minutes or so, until the vicar finally relented. His parting shot to me was that as the minister he was in charge of the church and that it was his responsibility to convene. Only his. He was emphatic that the marriage ceremony was not to be diminished.

"It is a sacred service and should not be taken lightly. The couple and myself are key players and the guests are witnesses. I take it very seriously indeed. This, not photos, flowers and videos, is the important issue."

I agreed with most of his sentiment. None of this was in dispute. It was simply his lack of understanding in embracing the outside world of HIS clients, the parishioners on the most important day of their lives. I failed to see how a well behaved video cameraman would upset the sanctity of the wedding and told him so bluntly. Finally, Jay came over and asked if it was alright to proceed. I assured him it would be and added that if he had any future problems with the Rev, to come outside and let me know. The minister heard every word as I added that I would be at the church entry waiting to check the arrival of the wedding party, anyway.

This had not been my original intent, but since I had been delayed in finishing the clear up, multi-tasking whilst arguing with the Rev, I would put the tools in the van and hang around to see Maggie in her finery. I hoped the day would go well. Goodness knows I was trying hard enough to ensure it would….

Technically, my remit was over now. Every single item on this agenda had been done. Earlier that day I had personally delivered all the bouquets to Maggie at her mum's house and watched her reaction. It was a typical one for her.

"Oh, my goodness! Look at this," and she lifted, like a brand newborn baby, her bouquet of white lilies interspersed with gypsophilia. The floral fashion at that time was trending to large, flowing bouquets for brides. There was lots of variegated greenery, too. Of course, Maggie had wanted the ultimate, the apogee of this style and had proffered a magazine photo of Mariah Carey at one of her many weddings, holding a massive creation. It was ginormous and Maggie wanted it – badly. "Just like this," I was told, "only even bigger!"

It was a remarkable bouquet and I was proud of the work that had gone into it. It was not just visually striking but engineered beautifully too.

162

Bouquets had to not only look good, they had to hold together without shredding all over the aisle floor. This was indeed a challenge for the florist.

The bouquet deliveries always gave me a chance to keep track of the smoothness of the day. It was important that I could, and invariably I would oblige with last minute emergencies – not just wedding related, but domestic – like popping down to the corner shop for milk, helping to throw together bacon butties and definitely making sure the floral deliveries were stored properly. It always upset me that the first choice for most folk would be the bathroom. No. A hot, steamy, busy, small bathroom is not a good place for fresh bouquets on the day.

"Remember to give these flowers a misting through the morning," were my last words to the chief bridesmaid as I left the family home where all the flowers were sensibly stored in the coolest area of the house. This happened to be a huge walk-in cupboard in the utility room. I had even left a special spray bottle of cold water to mist the blooms, for it had to be done delicately. Soaking was not an option and could result in causing the excess water to spill all over the dresses.

I was happy that my job of helping to create a great day was almost complete, so now it was good to just stand outside the church gates and await the main party. Nobody, not even a guest, had arrived yet although there were a couple of passers-by who had put down their shopping bags in anticipation of the action. They must have had keen instincts for no member of the wedding party had arrived yet. There were no limos or confetti to give the show away, but somehow they sniffed a wedding. People loved to watch all the goings-on at church weddings, although the arrival of the bride was really the main event. It was already almost half past two so the groom and best man would be here at any minute.

Sure enough, the silver Mercedes soon glided into the tiny car park in front of the gates and I expected to see the groom and best man exit, hopefully with their kilts fitting nicely. Mysteriously there were no passengers, only the excited chauffeur was in the car. It was big Ben and his face was frowning and pale with anxiety.

"I'm glad you're here, 'cos I just don't know what to do. When I went round to the groom's house there was nobody there – I rang and rang the bell. That was about quarter past two and I knew I was a bit early so I thought I'd give it more time and waited outside for him to appear – but no show at all. What happens now, eh?"

My empty, lunch-free stomach began to churn thinking of all the things that could go belly-up regarding our griping groom Hughie. Was he about to let Maggie down? Surely, even for him, that would be a no-no. I tried to think fast.

"Ben, go back up there." Fortunately the couple's home was only five minutes away. "Check again. If no joy, ask the neighbours where he might be…." I bit my bottom lip just thinking about the possibilities. "But I'd bet my last fiver he's in the pub with the best man. Find out which pub and then go down and get them out of there…fast!"

There are times when you do not wish to be right but unfortunately my swirling gut was correct. Ben found out from the vigilant house next door that our reluctant groom and his best man Drew were indeed down the Black Abbot Inn, his local esteemed and frequent hangout. It was obvious to the chauffeur that the two had been setting about their favourite hobby in an exacting fashion, bearing in mind the limited time slot before Hughie's wedding appointment.

Now back at the church, Ben abandoned them in the Mercedes for a moment in order to fill me in. The little group of spectators outside the church had grown considerably and they were about to get more entertainment than they had bargained for.

"They're both skunk-drunk. When I got to the pub I had to literally drag them out of there. I really think they had forgotten entirely about the wedding. But one blessing, they were at least in their wedding gear and it was a good thing they'd got dressed while they were still sober. They couldna' handle getting all that fancy kilt stuff on now, in their state. No way…"

I marched over to the Mercedes and pulled open the door angrily. Perhaps it is best not to repeat here what I said to them for I was furious – an anger that was aimed just as much at Drew the best man. Drew had sidestepped his responsibility to ensure his pal was organized that day – to get him to the church on time. Just like the song in the musical. The best man was well aware that Hangover Hughie would have required special help and Drunken Drew had absolutely not been the person to provide it. For the umpteenth time I thought of poor Maggie. Did she really want to marry this idiot, should I dissuade her?

I realized just how personally involved I had become in this wedding. I was not a family member, I told myself. Of course the bride had to already know what she was taking on with Horrible Hughie – surely? I suddenly realized I was grateful for ONE thing – the copious list of ghastly adjectives beginning with 'H' and 'D'. Seriously, was she so desperate to wear her beautiful, longed-for meringue? Was it worth it? Was it worth it to live a form of low life with, as I looked at his lifeless glassy eyes, a sub standard drunken moron?

The two idiots were frozen in their inebriated coma, incapable of responding to my tirade or making any move to exit the car. I slammed shut the heavy car door in frustration. I would speak to the Rev Warren about all this. I had realised that a legal ceremony like a wedding just might not be legal enough if the chief participants were stone drunk. Yes, maybe that self-righteous vicar who is so worried about flowers and videos could get a load of this…

Big Ben grabbed my arm, holding me back. "Remember, I have to go to the bride's mum's house now to pick up the bridesmaids in this Mercedes." He pointed a thumb in the direction of his vehicle. "So they – the two eejits inside – they've got to get out first, huh?"

Of course. I had lost my focus, blinded as I was with anger. "Hold on a couple more minutes,

Ben. I'm not sure where we are with all this. I mean, can these two even WALK?"

He frowned. "You're right. They could hardly put one leg in front of the other when I dragged them out of the pub…I had to practically carry them into the car."

Ben had the gigantic frame of his namesake, Ben Nevis. He stood at over six feet four and was broad and bulky with it. I hadn't chosen him as a chauffeur for this reason but sometimes his immense stature came in handy. On days like these.

"You had to DRAG them?" Why was I surprised….

"You betcha. When I say that I mean it. I feel sorry for this poor wee lassie whoever she is. I'm glad she's not my daughter!"

"She's called Maggie," I responded distractedly, and urged Ben to help me get the two imbeciles out of the car and over to the half wall, topped by iron railings just a few metres from the church gates. I would leave them to partially sit and lean against it while I fetched the preacher man.

Normally I was a stickler for scheduling at a wedding but this time I urged Ben not to rush back here with the bridesmaids. "And tell the Rolls' driver to go easy, too."

The Rolls Royce was always exclusively for the bride and would be already parked outside her mum's house, waiting for the timed slot to transport her to the ceremony.

"The bride can be fashionably late, that would suit all of us." I could imagine the Rolls' driver Archie's reaction as he was instructed to hold back and try to be late. Archie was always particular about his work and followed instructions to the letter since normally every minute mattered.

I left the drunks flopping against the wall like jaded puppets on broken strings and revisited Mr. Warren inside. Of course, he was still fussing around poor Jay, practically bullying him about his video routine all of which threatened to detain him from capturing on film the glorious, staggering arrival of the boozy bridegroom. Jay made his escape outside as I asked the minister to follow me to the car park where we actually NEEDED ecclesiastical guidance on what to do. I pointed out his next clients to him, the bar-fly Hughie and his best man.

"Here he is Rev Warren," I announced with a flourish as I walked over to the little makeshift bar stool of a wall. Amazingly, the two drunks were still semi perched on it and not on the ground as I had half-expected. Neither Hughie nor Drew looked ashamed, being just too gone to look anything other than plain drunk. Our outside audience had increased multifold, so much so we could have sold tickets. I mentally stored a plan to eventually shoo everyone back to make room in front of the church for the rest of the limos which were scheduled to arrive shortly.

The church minister's reaction was surprising. Shocking, even. I had asked him if, in view of their condition, it would still be alright – and legal - to continue with the marriage ceremony. He opted to ignore me.

"Can you walk?" he spoke to the bombed groom relatively calmly, as if he was a normal, sane individual. Dozy Drew was being ignored for now.

There was no formal reply, simply incoherent mumbling. Suddenly Hughie slid to the ground, the attempt at communication and speech obviously overwhelming him. In an attempt to save him, Drew landed on the ground too, joining him in the hangover party. It was an utter disgrace – at least, I thought so.

"So what do you make of this, Mr Warren? Is it still alright to proceed here? You can see how incapably drunk they are!"

Rev Warren shook his head disapprovingly but as I awaited his answer I spied the bridesmaids' Mercedes which was now attempting to enter our exciting and overcrowded little car park. Whilst the photographer busied himself with the girls' arrival photos, battle continued. The bridesmaids looked to be so wrapped up in themselves, I'm sure they never noticed the ensuing drama around the groom, but Rev Warren's response almost prompted me to fall in front of the limo.

"Well, they are definitely under the influence of alcohol, to be sure. But if they can walk down the aisle and make it through the wedding ceremony I see no reason to thwart the proceedings..."

I wanted to object but restrained myself. Deep down I knew this was wrong, for if these two gentlemen were not in control of their actions how could they participate in a sacred and legal ceremony? My gut instinct was that there should be no wedding here today although that thought came very uneasily. I had worked my tail off to put all this together for Maggie because I knew how much it meant to her. I had to bite my tongue to prevent myself from advocating that it should be called off entirely.

This was to be her dream day and I wanted her to have the fairytale she had longed for. But not this way. The wedding was one day, whilst Hungover Hughie was possibly FOREVER. He was a career drunk and he was quite uncommitted to her, which was obvious. God, this was so not my responsibility. I was supposed to be a coordinator, not a counsellor. It was really not appropriate, in spite of the overwhelming circumstances, for me to approve or otherwise but perhaps I had secretly hoped that the Rev Warren, who seemed to disapprove of EVERYTHING, particularly the minutia of the wedding, would step up to the plate and give the groom a jolly good ticking off, by refusing to officiate. And then...?

Well, then we would all go home and Maggie would see sense and get over it. That was one scenario.

The other was Rev Warren lecturing and bringing the groom to his immature senses, thereby sobering him up. After this Hughie would repent, vow to shun the demon drink and then we would all live happily ever after. Or not.

The truth is, it was a no win situation and devastating to the bride no matter what the attitude of the preacher man.

Rev Warren disappeared for a minute, then returned with two hefty janitors who each took a kilted drunk and helped him inside for the religious ceremony as the crowd looked on aghast. Perhaps the dipsomaniacs would be helped with strong tea or black coffee but no matter. I still felt devastated by the clerical response. That was it? I had decided to say nothing to the bride now but I did have a final word with Rev Warren. My earlier arguments with him suddenly seemed petty compared to this, this indecent act of treachery.

The minister was still outside chatting to a member of the crowd and he seemed to be quite unruffled by the flimflam. I cut in, to add my tuppence worth.

"Mr. Warren, I have to say it's interesting that you set much store by flower and video placement – like we saw inside earlier today. But what about the major ones – like marrying a couple when the groom is severely incapacitated? That reeks of impropriety and hypocrisy – no?"

I thought he might ask me how I REALLY felt. It was clear by his expression that there was an internal struggle going on, yet he offered little response.

"I'm sorry you feel that way," was all he said in reply. His face showed embarrassment but there was no explanation of his actions, no hint of just why he had chosen to go ahead with this sacrilegious scam.

He was so unflinching I began to wonder if perhaps I was being unfair and harsh in my criticism of him. Was I just disappointed that HE had decided not to bear the burden of denying this couple their wedding? Maybe I had just wanted to shift the weighty decision onto his shoulders, rather than take courage and appeal to the bride herself – for Maggie's face constantly haunted me. That was the hard part.

The Mercedes had emptied itself of the bridesmaids by now and had moved away to the little side car park. I appealed to the swelling crowd to move back a little for the Rolls Royce which would soon arrive and demand lots of space. Within minutes a cheer went up as the elegant bridal car came into view and soon Maggie was having pictures taken in her beautiful, elegant carriage, glowing and as happy a bride as I had ever seen. She waved as she noticed me near the gates and a zillion perplexing thoughts jetted through my mind. I digested her wide grin, her confident pose beside her brother who was giving her away and her mother, who had opted for the new fashion of travelling to the church with her daughter.

I truly ached for this poor bride and felt torn. Part of me wanted to yell, "Don't do it Maggie, just forget him! Go home and let it be!"

I determined to stay silent because I knew it was no use. That Hughie was a drunken lout would not have been earth shattering news for her. Also, by tolerating it, I believed she condoned it. After all, Rev Warren practically condoned it.

The bride made an attempt to gather up her train and get out of the car as her brother, already standing outside, took her hand. The photographer wanted all three at the front entry of the church for more photos before they went in. Before the ceremony. Before poor Maggie would commit her life away to her stewed, hapless groom…

It could have been the vision of Maggie basking in the limelight of her fake reality, her dreams about to be drowned and saddened by beer and whisky, for on impulse I dashed towards the Rolls and grabbed the bride's smooth bare arm under her sparkly veil before she exited the Rolls.

Every part of her seemed to be shimmering and I was about to de-glitz her whole day. I didn't stop for breath and as my tarnishing words rapid fired at her, her large, blue, professionally made-up eyes were filled with amazement.

"Maggie! You have to know this. Hughie is in there but we had to drag him out of the pub to get here and he's as drunk as a lord! Totally out of the game! Absolutely legless! So you have to decide if you want to go ahead with…" I finally exhaled, gesticulating towards the quaint, historic little church, the enthusiastic crowd, the whole ambiance of the wedding, "all this…"

She was very calm and turned to her mother, still sitting beside her in the car. "What do you think, Mum?"

Her mother looked very sad for a moment and shook her head knowingly. "This isn't that surprising, is it love? Did you really expect anything else? It's not too late to turn back. But it's your life, your decision and whatever you want, I'll have to back you up."

Even her mum. Et tu Brute. But by this time I was almost un-shockable.

Maggie turned back to ask: "Is he really so legless he can't walk? How did he get down the aisle?"

I explained that two heavies had to assist, which did not appear to upset her at all.

"Okay, so he DID make it down through the church? That's fine." She threw back her head determinedly. "Let's get on with the show."

Her brother had been chatting to the photographer all this time and she called him back. She took his hand firmly. Then to the 'ooh's' and 'aah's' of the patient admiring crowd, made her way to the kirk steps for photographs before her final unmarried journey down the aisle to her beloved.

The wedding ceremony proceeded successfully, by all accounts. As the bride entered the church I left, glad to escape at the first poignant strains of Mendelssohn and quite overcome by the oppressive double standards of the whole scenario. I needed a pot of tea or even a glass of wine. Alcohol was a good thing. Sometimes.

I never did find out if the marriage lasted or what became of the couple. Perhaps Maggie succeeded in reforming her Prince Charming. Perhaps Hangover Hughie eventually became the Husband of the Year. Perhaps pigs managed to fly. I had grave doubts at the time, but who knows?

The String of Pearls

No one else was willing to open the dreaded door and fetch the mother of the bride out of her gloomy bedroom. No one else seemed up for the job of persuading Jeannie to put on her posh new hat and a smiling face, come out of the darkness and accompany her daughter to her wedding. Especially not her loving family.

I turned the door handle gently and closed my eyes for a few seconds to acclimate them to the intense darkness inside that room. The overwhelming blackness just echoed the pervading emotional bleakness but respecting the chosen dreariness of this sanctuary, I chose not to switch on the light. It was sad that such melancholy dreich managed to overpower the sunshiny brightness of outdoors. Even on this day. This sunny, shiny, sparkly wedding day. It was a struggle to distinguish anything or anyone inside until I heard a sudden shuffling movement. This was the clue that led my ears and my uncertain gaze towards the bed where she sat, stunned and silent, staring morosely into her own personal black space.

"Come on Mrs Naismith," I urged gently. It was reminiscent of waking a child from a beautiful sleep. "It's time to get into the bridal car and take Serena to her wedding. Your brother Charlie is here to give her away, so we're all waiting…"

I reached for her arm, clothed for this occasion in its violet silk-covered sleeve. She did not resist. She rose from the bed, picked up her barely visible hat and handbag from the bedside table and walked past me - blatantly incognizant of my presence - towards the door and back into the hallway and the light.

A year or so before it had all been so different for Jeannie Naismith and for the friends and family who surrounded her. Each time she arrived in our dress salon with the bride for wedding appointments we all knew we were in for a jolly time, for Jeannie Elizabeth Naismith was a personality and a half, certainly one of life's more engaging characters. The eldest of her three girls was first to be wed and all of us in the salon could decipher that she was planning to take in every exciting ounce of the occasion. No decisions about that wedding were made without this lady present. We discovered that she and her deceased husband Jock had had a very sparse wedding day themselves about thirty years before so it was hardly surprising she wanted to make sure her daughter enjoyed all the frills and extras she had missed. It seemed that nothing was too serious or too sacred as she teased Serena and her bridesmaid sisters with silly anecdotes of their childhood. They were an irreverent fun group, mum being the funniest one there. She impressed me as a born raconteur and who doesn't enjoy a good story well told? She tickled our funny bones with snippets of her own past - particularly when she had lived and worked in New York as a young woman. It was obvious that her time spent there was special – all the pleasant tidbits of her American life were doled out to us as we dealt with the wedding business in hand. One of the most nostalgic threads was her cigarette choice. An expensive imported American brand was what she enjoyed exclusively as she nipped outside the salon to light one up.

There were many stories of New York. There were many stories of everything. Life. Death. Her husband had died just a couple of years before and she spoke fondly and often about him, always in a lighthearted, entertaining way. I do not recall the cause of his death. Perhaps he died laughing…

"Jock never wore a kilt in his life, but he just might have given in for his lass's wedding," she reflected. Six main members of the wedding party were to sport kilts for the big occasion. "Mind you, I'm no' too sure he would have had the legs for it – they were white, short and hairy…"

On one rare occasion she was serious and disconsolate with us. She had been mentioning the passing of her husband.

"He was far too young to die. Only fifty-four. It was three years ago next month, in fact. It was a great shock, a great shock….."

"Aye, it's a pity he's not here to give you away, Serena. But your uncle Charlie will make sure you get down that aisle."

She looked slightly more cheered, turning to me as I pinned her daughter's dress at the back of the bodice.

"Her uncle is Charlie Jackson. You'll have heard of him…? He's my wee brother, the success of the family."

The position of 'father' for Serena's wedding had been handed over to Jeannie's brother Charlie. The whole family was extremely proud of this gentleman who had risen to the ranks of a world class football player and subsequent manager. It only took a few more minutes into the dress appointment for Jeannie to boast about his status in the sporting world and also fill us in on some family secrets – just cute secrets, not scandalous ones. The innocent tales about him as a boy set the whole salon giggling.

She spoke about the time the priest came to her childhood home when Charlie was about five.

"My mother fed him the usual tea and biscuits and we all listened to his stories about being good and going to mass and all the rest. Then she had to cut him short."

"She told him that her wee boy was lying sick in his bedroom and she would have to check on him. Well, wee Charlie really wasn't well, but I believe my mother might have just been desperate to get rid o' the priest, too! Och, you know what priests are like! Well the priest was not for budging. He said to my mother 'We shall all go to his bedside and pray for his recovery'. In the name of God, Charlie wasn't THAT bad. He only had a touch o' the cold."

"We all tiptoed into the bedroom and poor wee Charlie was lying sleeping, his bottle of Lucozade on the table next to him. As you know, when you're a wean, Lucozade cures everything, eh?"

"Well a week or so before all this there had been some deaths in the street and my mother had explained to our Charlie that the priests that were coming and going into all the houses were giving out the Last Rites…"

There was a huge explosion of laughter in the salon. We suspected what was coming.

"Aye, sure enough we were all down on our hunkers and praying away when poor wee Charlie woke up. I'll tell you, if five year-olds could have had strokes, he would have had one right there and then."

"Oh, Ma! Am I dead? Am I dead?"

"I can still hear his poor wee cries thinking he was getting the Last Rites. I felt that sorry for him but you couldn't help laughing about it either."

I personally did not meet Charlie until the wedding day when I arrived at the house to take the bride, her mum and uncle to the church. Forewarned vaguely by Serena that Jeannie was 'not well', I came early in order to help out with the preparation of outfits, most of them supplied by my salon. I was chief driver, too. I chauffeured occasionally when I was needed and this was one wedding where I had deliberately placed my own name on the booking sheet under 'Driver'.

But I was not aware of the complication with this delightful lady at that time. Serena and her sisters had been vague about everything so it was not until the big day itself that I discovered the other, dark side of Jeannie. It was tragic.

It is said that the journey, rather than the arrival is what flavours life and I suppose this was certainly true regarding Jeannie for she got a big kick out of the wedding build-up: all the plans, every morsel of the razzmatazz. She had an encouraging opinion on the lot, was rarely critical and generally supported her daughter on her choices of gowns, flowers, cars and the rest.

This was a 'package' wedding which meant my input was pretty intense. Coordinating the needs of any wedding requires personal interaction in spades and I got to know the family well before the actual day. Or I thought I did.

But this drastically declined woman now being cajoled out of a cheerless dark space to witness a fabulous family celebration she had enthusiastically helped to plan, was a stranger to me. It was shocking to see such dramatic change in an individual.

I paused for a few seconds and blinked at the brightness in the hallway. Jeannie was motionless, simply staring into space, the group of people around her obviously invisible, imperceptible.

"Are you alright Mum?" Serena could not hide her anxiety behind her gossamer fine veil but for now she would have to. Later on in the church she could lift back her tulle shield from her freckled face and perhaps – who knows – she would delight in seeing her mother's awful trough of torment just miraculously drain away. I believe she had this presentiment, as the rest of us who stood in that little hallway certainly did.

She squatted down just a speck to check her mum's deadpan expression more fully. Mrs. Naismith was already a few inches shorter AND she was wearing flat pumps while Serena had self-elevated an ambitious four inches via her smart satin bridal heels. Some reassurance was called for from the wedding specialist.

"She'll be fine," I said. "Just let's get the bridesmaids away from here straightaway in their

Mercedes. Then it's Mum and me first into the Rolls Royce, followed by you and your uncle."

It was military precision at this point. My job was to let each group grab their limelight individually as they headed from the house to the cars. If the family all left together it looked messy and disorganised for the outside onlookers, of which there were many. Both bridesmaids set off in their crisp, jade green taffeta dresses. As they approached their car our driver Gally opened the rear door and helped them in. All this was to a background of the crowd's cheers and yells and general happiness. I heard the car drive off and felt relieved that this first step was over.

Right. Now it was our turn. I turned Jeannie around slightly to face the little hall mirror and arranged her hat correctly. It was a charming concoction of mauve crystal organza layers and dotted with tiny fine velvet rosebuds. The design was very flattering to her features and the reddish gold colouring of her hair, similar to her three girls. She was mid-fifties and had a pleasant face. "Wi' no wrinkles!" she had told us all at the shop.

"No, I don't have wrinkles," she insisted. "They're just laughter lines."

Probably true.

She had told me about her wedding outfit some months ago when she was in the salon with Serena. The hat was the item she most looked forward to wearing.

"Have you ever heard the like? Do you know the hat cost more than the dress, shoes and bag combined? But I don't care because without it, the outfit just looks nothing at all."

Not a surprise. I had heard similar stories many times from many brides' mothers. Her dress was simple. Just a long-sleeved , drop-waisted silk chiffon floaty number, its length extended almost to the ankles. Again, she had already filled me in some weeks before.

"It's no' supposed to be full length but because I'm so wee it looks practically like a long frock. But you know, it's nice, really nice."

As I stood there with her in the hallway I realized she was spot on with her choice – it was very elegant. I was ready to tell her so because she looked perfect. Well, almost perfect. If it hadn't been for those pearls.

The delicate string of pearls around her neck looked amazing from the front but as I peered more closely at the back I noticed the malefactor. Because of the hat brim and her hairline it had almost escaped my notice – but yes, it was there alright. A large steel safety pin. It was perched incongruously between the catches at each end of the delicate strand of creamy white pearls. Almost imperceptible now, but in time everyone would have to be blind not to notice. Especially later on at the reception on removal of the hat. I quietly pointed the problem out to Serena.

"Oh, no! Those are the pearls Dad gave her before he died – I think it was their anniversary. God, Mum loves them. She was always supposed to wear them but we kept having problems with the clasp – it's difficult to work it, you know? So last week we just bought her a new strand."

Serena was becoming quite agitated and at this stage of the proceedings, as she was almost about to leave for her wedding, I understood her tension.

"Where are they…? What has she done with the new ones – are they still in the bedroom? Could someone go in and have a look?"

I studied the pearls more closely and tried to reassure the bride.

"I don't think there's anything wrong with the pearls she's wearing, Serena. I'm sure if we take the safety pin off I can work the clasp and get them around her neck easily enough."

I was relieved that I had come over here early. I knew that if we didn't get a move on, this wedding would run late. Not a good thing at all. We still had a few minutes up our sleeves if we moved calmly. Between us we removed the nostalgic anniversary heirloom from the Naismith neck and unfastened that awful safety pin. The catch was a bit tricky but I managed to secure it and the pearls back onto their silent, still glum wearer.

Serena was trying to make sense of it all. She shook her head so rapidly I was afraid her headdress would land on the floor. "It just shows you. She's supposed to be totally out of it and yet she managed to find my dad's pearls that we had hidden away. PLUS she was determined to get them on, even with a safety pin. No shiny new ones for her."

Then the anxious bride turned to me hopefully.

"Do you think that's a good sign? I mean – just the idea of her even thinking about jewellery. She's shown no interest in anything for weeks now."

Of course I wanted to say it was a great sign. But I was a wedding specialist, not a psychologist. Thankfully I had no real experience of depression or bi-polar patterns so I was not in a position to comment.

"Could be…." It was uncomfortable discussing Jeannie as if she were not there, but I tried to sound positive. It was clearly enough reassurance for Serena whose eyes seemed to take on a fresh brightness, even behind the handy shelter of her veil.

"Right! Let's get the show on the road here. Serena…just take a deep breath and come outside smiling in about two minutes with Uncle Charlie. I'll get this lovely, elegant, be-pearled lady into our lovely, elegant Rolls and wait for elegant you to join us. Now, remember…smile!"

I put on an exaggerated Cheshire cat grin to illustrate the point. It was a good mantra for all our brides. Relax. Smile. Smile even if you trip up going down the aisle. Even if your feet ache, smile….I wish I could have made Jeannie Naismith smile just then. I wanted her to sparkle and radiate joy again. I knew that deep down she could be that other, better person. Just not today. Sadly, just not on the biggest, most important day of her daughter's life.

I turned to Charlie. "Your sister will be in the back of the car waiting for Serena and you will be in the front passenger seat with me, ok?" I threw

190

in a tiny tease. "And remember to lock the door behind you. You're the last one out to face the crowds. You should smile, too!"

He grinned at my bossiness, but I knew Charlie Jackson could manage. He had faced bigger crowds than this. A hundred or so neighbours outside might have overawed Serena and her folks, but it would have no effect on him, the football idol of millions. The truth was it was he, not the bride, who was the main attraction for the massive throng outside. Everyone wanted to see Serena, of course. That was a given. But it was not every day that they got to see a local hero, a world-class football legend like Charlie Jackson up close.

For his niece's big day he had stepped away from his now wealthy, prestigious environment in Helensburgh and back into the working-class society of his youth – to the rows upon rows of council homes in a modest area of Glasgow's east end suburbs. It was here he had cut his teeth on the finesse of kicking and handling a football on the streets. And now he was back home to receive accolades from 'his ain folk' who respected and loved him just as much for his family values as his ability with a ball. Charlie had never been a 'flash' footballer dashing around nightclubs with babes on his arm. There had been none of that type of nonsense with him. Just a lovely wife, kids and a brilliant career.

I lead the way out to open the car doors and took Jeannie's arm.

"You look gorgeous, Mrs Naismith!" These were the shouts of some teenagers.

"Och, the bride must be jealous, Jeannie," yelled a neighbour. "You look a million dollars, so you do."

The compliments flew in from every direction although Jeannie seemed oblivious to them all. Several longtime friends and neighbours came forward to hug her lovingly or just take her hand gently. Perhaps they were hoping to retrieve her spirit out of the blackness. There was a great empathy for her and I could feel it as I walked with her. In communities like these, people's happiness and pain seemed to network themselves. Everyone appeared to know what Jeannie was going through and they were riding the wave with her.

After the dapper Mrs Naismith got into the rear of the Rolls I held both doors open for our final passengers who were just leaving the house. Immediately a gigantic cheer went up from a mixed group of women, men and children. There

192

were people perched on each other's shoulders, either sitting or standing on fences and garden gates, waving football scarves. It was not often men showed interest in a neighbourhood wedding but this was different. This was Charlie Jackson. Some wee boys tried to clap which wasn't easy, for holding a football under your arm makes clapping unworkable.

Serena smiled and waved, soaking up the atmosphere. She would have had no illusions about the mixed loyalties of the spectators but it was clearly immaterial. She was still the bride after all. She was able to show off her beautiful dress, her perfect make-up and hair – and her famous uncle. It was all part of the parade. She clambered up into the limo beside her mum as Charlie performed a special role for the spectators, particularly the younger ones.

He took a large bag of coins from his sporran and threw them wildly down into the crowd, into the street and away from the car itself. This was the completion of the 'scramble' – a Scottish wedding tradition I occasionally loathed. It could be dangerous and slow. The secret was to toss those coins, a good luck gesture, well away from where the car was headed, avoiding accidents. Children would dive under a car wheel for fifty pence so it was crucial to 'scramble' safely. I would not

drive away until I absolutely knew it was safe.
Charlie was an ace. He managed it beautifully
sending the kids in the crowd well away from our
wheels and off down the other end of the street.
Finally he jumped into the passenger seat as I
checked for stray kids.

"It's not nice to run over children with your Rolls
Royce," I joked as I got into the driver's seat.
"I'm sure you never do that with yours, eh?" He
laughed as we set off slowly, very slowly,
allowing the crowds outside time to see and cheer.

It was a short five minute drive to the church.
After some photos with the cars themselves, the
vehicles and the chauffeurs would leave. This
was not a normal situation, but since the wedding
was to be in the adjacent church hall, no
transportation or limos were required after the
ceremony. Then, the wedding party and guests
would simply walk across the car park to the
parish hall tucked tidily amongst a handsome
garden full of flowers, shrubs and evergreen trees.

"We'll have the photographer take plenty of pics
with the cars, Serena." I peered at her in my rear-
view mirror. "Before we drive them off, I mean.
Bridesmaids, too. They'll be waiting for you at
the church steps."

She nodded and turned to her mother. "We'll have to get photos of you with the wedding cars as well, Mum. And maybe a few sitting in it, eh? So make sure you just stay by me and Charlie for a wee while."

Jeannie still clinged to her comatose state – there was no reaction whatsoever to her daughter's words.

I pulled the big silver Rolls right up to the foot of the church steps and parked for the photo opportunity. I hoped this wouldn't take too long for it was only five minutes until the ceremony and of course the photographer would want to milk his chance to snap away with the limos in the background. Schedules, schedules….I realized I was over reacting. After all, the reception was right here afterwards, only ten paces away with no drives to locations or hotels. Yes, weddings like this were much easier to timetable.

The wedding party was shuffled around like a pack of cards, assuming various poses and controlled by Kenny, one of our team photographers. He knew we were a tad late so he wasted no time rallying the group together for photos.

"Just the bride and her Dad!" he yelled.

I squirmed. I assume other people there squirmed, too.

I had a quick word in his ear. "It's not her Dad. I told you this and the family told you, too. It's her uncle, and it's Charlie Jackson, for God's sake. Do you not recognize him?"

It was Kenny's turn to squirm.

"No. I'm sorry. I'm not a football fan, but yeah, I've heard of him. He's pretty major, isn't he?"

I backed off in disbelief and let him get on with the job in hand.

"Just the bride and uncle beside the Rolls!" he corrected, turning sheepishly in my direction. "Nobody else!" He bawled roughly and loudly.

Perhaps he was just trying to be authoritative and self-assured after his faux-pas…..

"No," I told myself reluctantly. "No, he was being rough and loud."

Whatever. But what Jeannie did in response to his cry was pretty awesome.

She seemed to emerge almost defiantly from her deep coma of gloom. Totally defying his command, she walked briskly to the bridal car, stepped up between the shocked, but beaming Serena and her uncle and elbowed her beloved hero-brother Charlie right out of the way. Right out of the picture entirely. She stood there determinedly and steadied herself for the photo. I searched her face anxiously for an expression of real emotion – hopefully joy. There seemed to be none.

The only body language came from her gloved right hand which she moved up towards her neck, seeming to search urgently for those creamy white pearls. The anniversary pearls from her beloved deceased husband Jock. But just then, as she touched them gently and sighed, I observed the faintest shadow of an enigmatic smile…...

Then she turned slightly, still caressing those pearls, towards the photographer.

Boris Bachmann and Other Barracudas

"I find it rather easy to portray a businessman. Being bland, rather cruel and incompetent comes naturally to me."

John Cleese

I slammed the phone down so violently, so murderously, that when it rang for the second time I jumped back, shocked that it was still alive. God! I wish I HAD actually killed the wretched thing, because I knew that this fresh call would be an encore from Boris. Crass and brazen as ever, naturally he was phoning back. He was still audaciously attempting to cajole me into helping him out with MY wedding cars for HIS wedding car company for the following weekend, even though he knew my limited patience with him had already fizzled out. I picked up.

"Look, Boris. The reality is your reputation in business stinks. You owe me three hundred pounds from way back, months ago. Unless that's paid in cash, upfront, and accompanied by a FULL prepayment of this new wedding – then there will be no other jobs. EVER! Okay?"

"Darling, daa-aa-rling. Of course." He was so sleazy. How blood actually crawls I am not sure but I do know that just then my blood felt as if it was crawling – and boiling, like Vesuvius ready to erupt.

"Of course I'll pay you, sweetie. My chauffeur will have a big fat envelope to give your chief driver next Friday. No problem."

"No way, daa-aa-rling." I could fake sleazy if I had to. "I need all monies paid at least three days before, in cash. I don't trust your cheques anymore than I trust you. Got it?"

"But, daaa-aaa-rling…"

"That's the deal, Boris. Take it or leave it. If you decide to take it I want the money at the shop by Monday or Tuesday at the absolute latest. I'll instruct my staff to call me the moment you deliver it. Until then, no formal arrangements have been sealed, so your wedding is at risk. Goodbye."

I slammed the poor little beige instrument down again onto its long-suffering cradle with the brute force of Attila the Hun. God, that man! He was a real pain in the……

I wondered why I had ever had anything to do with him in the first place. He was as unscrupulous as they come, a creature totally devoid of one single redeeming feature. Every limo supplier in my wonderful world of weddings knew it, too.

Our tumultuous relationship went back a few years. Boris had contacted me when my company was still growing – when I had only a couple of Mercedes in my fleet and had to subcontract Daimlers and Rolls Royce from other firms to suit my customers' requirements. He was at that time the owner of a highfalutin', extensively advertised limo hire company in Paisley, near the city airport and needed little people like me to bolster his fleet. Like the big bad wolf he subsequently proved himself to be, he would sit in his silk suit in his swish office and try to call all the shots. He was actively seeking innocent young companies like my own to come on board with hard won, professionally chauffeured cars for weekend work. I was impressed at that time that he would honour me by subcontracting my lowly vehicles since he really put himself on a big, gold, glitzy - and as I later found out - greasy pedestal. You could say that in the world of wedding cars, Boris was a professional predator and abuser....

It all worked well for a time. It meant I did not have to upkeep huge classic cars for a short season of weddings. Instead I could contract them from Boris, whose inventory of vehicles seemed endless. I never did get involved in corporate work – cushy airport pickups and the like, so those two Mercedes of mine had to work a little harder to cover their keep. They would be hired out to other small businesses like my own – and occasionally to Boris. The majority of companies we dealt with were straightforward and honest. We helped each other out and we paid each other accordingly since it made a lot of sense to do the honourable thing. It meant I could pick up a phone and order one or two cars easily, if they were available, from the limo community. They would do the same with me, for this section of the wedding business community it was good, honest, smart business. The added bonus of contracted work from such an important firm excited me as it did many other small limo businesses so we naively felt quite important in the beginning. Of course we were all being groomed for Boris's evil empire.

Boris was a different breed. Oh, he started well enough. After he contacted me in the early days he did not put a foot wrong, at first. He took care of his obligations and I was happy. But his demonic personality could not be hidden for long and soon he would become forgetful about such details. As more and more limo companies abandoned him his financial problems soared, leaving him with a chunk of his fleet repossessed. He disappeared for a while in shame, the rumour circulating that he had absconded to London. Poor old London. They'd already had the Blitz. Now they had Boris. Of course he eventually resurfaced on the Scottish wedding scene practically begging hopefully-amnesic associates for help with his bookings.

This is where we were when he audaciously called me. I knew that others would have turned him down flat since he owed everyone money, so I decided to take advantage of his current helplessness to recover my debt. If he needed cars so badly then I would make him square up. Yes, prepay would save the day...

He did come into the shop a few days later and settled his bills meekly and politely, according to the staff. Hmmm. I still did not trust him, but I knew that by doing this wedding for him, at least some poor unsuspecting couple would not be let down. This was the danger he diced with every time he refused to play ball. He had no empathy for his clients - as the multitude of Boris stories permeating the wedding game circuit will back up.

I wondered how long it would be before Boris would be naughty again and decided he would double-cross that bridge when he came to it. To think I tried to impress this hustler the first time we met. I recalled that after his initial call to introduce his company some years before, I had set off, like a lamb to the slaughter, all the way into Paisley to see the man personally - and I was pretty nervous. I was a small potato in the suburbs enjoying being treated courteously by him as he lounged in his leather swivel chair in his expensive office. He was charming, if a bit oily in his manner. An unmarried fifty-something, he wore slim fitting Italian silk suits and slicked back his mousy hair, conjuring up a sixties' Hollywood image of the mafia. As I sat down across from him at his opulent mahogany desk I fully expected him to make me an offer I couldn't refuse. Which, of course, is exactly what he did.

I had a few gaps in my diary over the next few months and he filled them in for me. Good. Cars lying around idle and without weddings were useless, and expensive. Better for them to be working. Of course I was happy to make business contact with such a big important company, ingenue that I was. Okay, so he looked a bit like an elderly Michael Corleone, so what? He had work for me, work for my drivers, so it was all good.

I shook his little limp manicured hand and left. As we said goodbye I half-expected him to tell me to take the cannolis. He did not. But as I was to ultimately learn, Boris absolutely never gave away any freebies….

Our subsequent relationship was an interesting one, for the stories of Boris were legendary. I must admit I enjoyed chauffeuring at some of his weddings, usually in Glasgow, where the other drivers would spill the beans on the man himself and his wily ways. Often the gossipers were his own employees – or occasionally they were from an outside company which had previously suffered at the hands of Boris the Barracuda. I often wondered why they were still involved with him, but they were. Perhaps it was a case of 'keep your friends close and your enemies closer'.

"I used to house three of my cars at his depot in Paisley. He was charging me so little I just had to go along with the programme," a bitter Boris victim told me one day as we were out chauffeuring at a wedding.

John Innes was a young man who ran a small car company from his home in Paisley. Since Boris had a large warehouse fairly nearby, next to the city airport, this sounded like an excellent arrangement. Parking and storage were always issues for small limo companies. I struggled myself latterly, once the limo fleet had expanded.

He continued with a typical, painful Boris tale. "I did this for almost a year. One weekend I went wi' a couple of my drivers to his warehouse to uplift my cars for our weddings. Boris wasn't there but a lad who worked for him gave me some advice."

"He said, 'You seem like a decent bloke. Take my advice, don't leave your cars here any more. Bachmann is using them midweek for his corporate driving. Honest.' Would you credit it? And he was charging ME to garage the cars there..."

"Well, that was it. I couldn't really prove it, but knowing Boris he would have been adjusting the clocked mileage to cover his tracks. The lad would have been right enough, 'cos we all know Boris has no scruples. He'd flog his granny for two pence, no mistake. I only do jobs for him now at inflated rates, take it or leave it. He's got so few good contacts now, he mostly has to take it."

My sentiments exactly.

The stories were so audacious, we had to laugh, trying not to dwell on Boris's poor, innocent customers who inevitably suffered at his hands. They would not have appreciated the humour in our tittle tattle. John Innes was fired up by this time and highlighted another stunt Boris pulled with his own customers.

"The guy at Boris's place filled me in on another story. He told me the boss himself was showing one of my Mercedes. I'd forgotten to take out my baby's seat in the back and there was Boris showing the car off to a punter. He looked shocked to see the baby seat but quick as a flash he reacted. 'Well, as you can see we cater for everyone, even babies.' Gotta give him full marks for thinking fast, eh?"

A favourite stunt pulled by Boris was known in the limo business as 'doubling up'. The idea was to take one wedding party to their church service - Catholic weddings preferably since their religious ceremonies generally took much longer, especially a full mass. After his drivers dropped off their passengers at the first event, they would scarper off to another wedding entirely to transport THEM to either the church or reception. Then they would go back to the first. If they made it in time they would assist in getting everyone to the reception. Subsequent to this, back again to the second wedding. Get the idea? I get dizzy just thinking about it….

This was great for Boris, if it worked. But it rarely did without repercussions. Although he would collect two wedding fees for the afternoon instead of one - like the rest of us normally did - the chances of carrying this off were practically zero. Most weddings were at the magic hour of three o'clock. Such a time offered continuity for a reception meal at five-thirty or six o'clock. So with the same schedule, every wedding needed cars at the same time, right? This is why people paid expensive prices for these limos, since they were exclusively for weddings happening just once daily and only on weekend afternoons. Boris set out, greedily and delusionally, to change all that.

If this practice had been workable, believe me, many of us might have employed it. But it was not. No one dared try to double up - only Boris was underhanded enough to go there. He let many young couples down and everyone in the wedding car business was amazed that, because of this one sin above all others, he survived in business as long as he did. One experienced Lanarkshire businessman explained to me how he had recently been duped by Boris. It was amazing how many of us were conned. I hadn't seen middle-aged Walt Johnson for a while when we shared a wedding job in Largs, Ayshire. If the conversation between drivers became dull, we switched over to Boris stories.

"I did a wedding for him in Greenock last month. I was the third car, a Mercedes, along with Boris's Rolls and Mercedes," said Walt. "After we dropped all the party off at the church, the other two cars took off to another wedding. Just like that. We were all supposed to wait, of course, to take everybody to the reception but I was all on my own. The chief driver, the Rolls guy, he told me not to worry and that they would only be a half-hour."

"They never came back and the family was furious. They were asking where the cars were, so what could I do? I had to shuttle the bride and groom and the best man then come back for the three bridesmaids, with a final run for the parents. The work of three cars, which the punters had paid for. They knew it wasn't my fault, like. I billed him for the extra runs but he hasn't paid me yet. But he will. Just wait…" Considering Walt was over six feet and annoyed, I feared for Boris's health.

The doozy of them all was the account from a gentleman who supplied horse-driven carriages. I met him at an 'un-Boris" affair in Cumbernauld and he was still seething over a recent painful experience with the Barracuda.

Old Joe MacDuff was based out in the country, having a small farm near Stirling and it was clear that he was very particular about his modus operandi regarding the welfare of his horses. He had several animals, apparently of varied stamina and transported them in a horsebox, with the carriage, to within the regulatory few hundred yards of the bride's address. He would then set up the fairytale carriage leaving his delivery vehicle parked safely until his return after the wedding. This way, the horses would not be subjected to long, tiresome rides because the distance between points – house to church, church to reception – were, for Joe, of great importance. To boot, his horse-driven carriage would normally be exclusively for the bride and her dad before the wedding and then only for the freshly married couple afterwards. This was all understandable stuff.

"I'll no' accept a job that isnae fair tae the horse," he told me resolutely. "The bride has tae be collected nae mair than a mile frae the kirk and the kirk has goat tae be nae mair than a mile frae the reception. Noo," he turned and glared at me as if I were the enemy, "I make that clear tae all my customers."

I understood perfectly. Not being a proud owner myself of horse-driven carriages, I often sub-contracted them for my clients, backed up by our limousines. So I was familiar with the geographical and equine limitations.

Joe straightened up his six feet plus frame while his honest, ruddy face displayed his displeasure.

"I didnae ken that this Boris wis a gangster, like. So I signed up for wan o' his joabs in Kirkintilloch. Whit a mistake that wis."

"Aye, it was fine getting tae the kirk, ken. But then the two back-up Mercedes jist nipped aff and left me, telling me they would be back in a few minutes. Back by the time the ceremony was over, like. Well, I was sweating blood in case they wid be late. Late! That wid hae been bad enough. Bejeez…they never came back at all."

"Ken, I had to dae a shuttle up and doon wi' a' the wedding party tae the reception. Poor Poseidon was aboot knackered by the time we'd finished. I had tae sponge him doon for ages efterwards – before I pit him in the van. Naw, I'll nivver dae another wedding wi' that crook again. Nivver. The miserable auld beast." He meant the horse. "Cruelty, it wis."

I commiserated with him about the hapless Poseidon.

"Ken, as bad as it wis – I was glad I hid decided to use Poseidon that day. He's my youngest horse." Old Joe stood up a little straighter yet again and even smiled fondly. "But my favourite horse is Hermes, he's the auldest o' the lot. If I had taken auld Hermes, that wid ha' bin a tragedy. He disnae move fast, dis Hermes."

I wondered, then, why he had been named after the Greek God of Speed. But then I thought of Harpocrates, the Greek god of silence, and kept my mouth shut.

"Aye, if it hid been Hermes, I wid jist have gone hame, wedding or no wedding. Taxis for the folks is whit I wid hiv said."

At least Boris contaminated, in his short reign, only wedding car business. For me personally, cars were only one slice of an expanding nuptial pie which fed my company by embracing every service – the main one being gowns for brides and bridesmaids. But there were aisles and aisles of barracudas in this area too. Their disreputable ways led, on a number of occasions, to our being a bridal dress SOS centre. A shelter for abandoned brides, so to speak.

Many times over my own decades of trading, a number of large, fancy, well-advertised wedding shops in the city centre went into liquidation leaving hundreds of brides, who had all paid upfront, sans their dresses and accessories. Such patterns of 'going out of business' meant they closed their doors without notice. Brides were then locked outdoors - their noses pressed against expensive plate glass bay windows in premier locations, as all their dreams were unfairly imprisoned inside. This was bad enough but it was even more despicable to learn that some brides had just ordered and paid for their dresses days or even hours before the liquidation - when the barracudas already knew that they could never deliver.

News like this flashed across television screens and for days our salon phone would ring off the hook with brides desperate to get dresses at short notice, for some of them were to be married within weeks. The situation was ridiculous and there must have been a host of honest salons like ours working overtime to get many of these young women sorted out. Of course most of the problems were sorted out eventually, but not before bevvies of brides paid the price with extra expense and heartache.

It was a touch annoying then to absorb the aftermath of all this chaos about a year or so later. The odd client of ours, when asked about choosing a wedding or bridesmaid dress from our wide selection as part of the package, for example, would occasionally decline, explaining, "I was going to get the dresses here, but there's a beautiful new shop just opened in Glasgow – a massive salon – and they're doing discount deals on dresses all this month! So I'm going there."

More than a few of these new fancy shops had happened to spring up just after the 'going into liquidation' companies had let so many girls down. What the clients never realized was that the owners of the new fancy salons were the same people who had abandoned ship before. We knew their strategy but the customers did not.

It tended to look a trifle sour-grapeish when something like this was found out. Our advice would have been to put down as small a deposit as you can – then when the ordered dress arrives in the salon get it home into your own wardrobe as soon as possible. If dresses needed alterations, as most of them do, arrange those asap also. Do not procrastinate. At all.

We might have added that if brides or bridesmaids DID intend to lose ten pounds or so of body weight, then to do so as quickly as possible for alterations purposes. But then again, it would have been fair comment to explain that anyone dealing with a barracuda wedding dress company would have likely found it easy to drop ten pounds or more. Stress always manages to take care of that. Oh, yes.

The Second Time Around

The irony of the whole situation was that Charlene, our no nonsense bride, had despised all the wedding fuss the first time. A second go was definitely not about to be a propitious prospect. But life does get in the way of plans, sometimes.

In my world, my reality, where female wedding clients occasionally invoked hissy fits and mental breakdowns over the colour of a piece of ribbon, Charlene Currie was a breath of fresh air.

This is not to say that she didn't care about her forthcoming wedding. She and her partner Callum simply had a more worldly, pragmatic approach to the whole wedding business and never allowed it to consume their every waking moment.

It would be dense for me to wish everyone had employed the same attitude for if this had been the case then my wedding shop would have been relegated bigtime. A visit to our nice salon might have taken on the lowly importance of popping over to the chippie or even dashing out to the ice-cream van in your slippers. No. Weddings were important. They absolutely were and that's why the majority of our clients rightly made it clear that this was the biggest day of their lives.

At our first introductory appointment Charlene and Callum were a teensy bit abnormal by briefing me that they wanted their wedding day coordinated by my company so that they could get on with their already very happy lives right here and now and not have to spend a moment longer than necessary dealing with the fuss and frippery which special occasions demanded. Such an attitude was reasonable and the handing over of a wedding with minimum input from clients was perfectly understandable.

They were professionals – both architects – and when they were not honing the design of their prospective new marital home, they were off travelling to foreign exotic cities. It is safe to say the new glam home and the holidays were more attractive to this couple than a big flashy wedding. They had opted for a really long honeymoon, pooling their annual time off work into a one fell swoop six-week tour of Thailand, culminating in a splashy final two weeks on the naturally blonde beaches of Koh Samui enjoying watersports.

This was their big deal, not agonizing over ribbons, lace and Mendelssohn. I had a feeling that the minor preliminaries, such as getting married, were mere formalities to please the mums and dads. Obligingly, as always, I got on with the stuff of their wedding. Personally, I enjoyed the freedom of not having to look over my shoulder to ask about every little thing. Trust was a valuable commodity in the wedding game.

So, as the handsome couple filled the long winter evenings with advanced scuba diving classes, I got to work on the wedding. Their classes took place mainly at the local swimming baths and although I knew nothing about scuba science, my mind was boggling a little. I was trying to mentally equate the chlorine-laden cold pool in Scottish February with the balmy tropical and kaleidoscopically beautiful fish-laden waters of Thailand. Hardly the same thing.

It became even more ludicrous when a few weeks before the date Charlene came round for final fittings for her portfolio of hired dresses. I was keen to find out how the aqua pursuits were faring. As she slipped into her strappy, duchess satin gown, I was brought up to date.

"We're off to Loch Lomond next week to try the diving for real. It won't be like the South China Sea, of course, but it's still more authentic than the baths."

I nodded solemnly in agreement. Loch Lomond was beautiful for sure but I had never heard it compared - even slightly - to an exotic resort in Thailand. It struck me just then that perhaps the local baths held a stronger resemblance, after all.

"You know, I'm not sure just how deep Loch…" She stopped in mid-sentence as she glanced in the mirror and approved the look. "I really like this dress, very, very much. But I'm glad I'm just hiring it. What on earth would I do with it later?" She softened again. "Although it is lovely…."

Yes, even the toughest, most sensible dames fall for the Cinderella dress routine eventually. Sometimes I felt like the Fairy Godmother.

Other than the bridal outfit we provided fresh flowers, a cake, limos and the men's kilt outfits, plus bridesmaid dresses for both of her glamourous friends, Sandra and Tina. They were overjoyed with the jade satin sheath gowns which really contrasted well with the soft vanilla shade of the wedding gown itself.

"LOVE the bold shade of the dresses," said Sandra, an attractive brunette. "If we are only going to be two bridesmaids then we may as well stand out a little. Nothing pale and pretty for us, huh?"

Tina was a little quieter, but with her long thick auburn hair, the hue of the dress was a major compliment in every way. The bride could see how great she looked, too.

"Green is definitely your colour, no one suits it better than a redhead."

But Tina still looked a trifle nervous, much more so than our relaxed bride. She shared her concern with us.

"I think so too, girlfriends. But I told my gran about the dresses last weekend and she was a bit worried about the colours. She told me that. She said 'You know Tina, we used to say that at weddings, green should never be seen. It's supposed to be unlucky.' So do you think that's just an old wives' tale? Let's hope my gran's havering, for Charlene's sake!"

Charlene, of course, was not in the least put out.

"Oh, Tina! Of course it's an old wives' tale. Luck is what you make happen, that's what I was brought up to believe."

She immediately changed the nervous energy in the room. The girls laughed and all agreed that the granny talk was just nonsense.

"And you two are lucky enough to look fantastic. You're putting this old bride to shame here, don't stand so close in for the wedding line-up photos!"

The flower package allowed me to deliver the fresh bouquets to the bride at her mum's home on the day. The atmosphere was electric and I noticed that everything was perfectly organized as I arrived with the order. I felt it was surprisingly well underway in fact, for a three o'clock kick-off. Charlene was having her full make up done and it was not yet midday. Her mum was in the throes of getting into her finery and so were the bridesmaids, who were already made up and coiffed. I had an idea why everyone was so well prepared.

I even detected a frisson of excitement from the casual, sensible bride that morning. "The photographer will be here at one o'clock so we have to be ready," she informed me. "He suggested all these house pictures, so I thought why not?" Charlene really surprised me with this arrangement which seemed to be out of character for her. "You know, it'll spur things on a bit, too. We definitely won't be late for this three o'clock service."

I left the flowers safe and cool in the dining room and took off. Everywhere else was far too hot in that hopping house. The photo arrangements were nothing to do with us, for the couple had booked an outside company of their own choice. I was always slightly sceptical of this snapping set-up at home although I had experienced a good many brides who genuinely relished the idea of a photographer prowling around as they prepared for their busy wedding day. I wondered why a pragmatist like Charlene would opt for such an arrangement. Tripping over a camera as she reached out for her headdress or lipstick kind of went against the grain of this girl, yet she still went for preparation photos, nonetheless.

Like the majority of our weddings, this one was unremarkable in its normality. I set off to the church and reception to check all was well with cake and flowers, waved off the chauffeurs in the limos and then went back to the salon. Clockwork. The limos were on time, of course and the cake was delicious, for I was given a small piece to try later. Yes, just as weddings should be. If everything falls into place then we have no horror stories to tell our children or grandchildren. Unfortunately, we rarely relate tales of the ordinary – just the extraordinary.

This wedding would have been almost forgettable except - after the very extended six-week honeymoon a telephone call from Charlene had me puzzled. She was quite upset and insisted on seeing me as soon as possible. I told her to come straight over. There was no explanation, what on earth?

"It's the photos. They didn't turn out! We don't have any from the wedding – I just can't believe it!"

These were the days before digital photography, a science which is almost foolproof now. At the time, my own home camera was not, for me, a reliable source of recording family occasions. Taking photographs was a touch and go exercise when some results were fine and some disastrous. Unfortunately one never knew until the film eventually came back from the developing lab and we could find out the results via the chemist's shop. But, I reminded myself silently, I was an amateur. These unsuccessful pics had been snapped by a pro.

It was strange to see her so overwrought, for the Charlene we knew was generally calmness

222

personified. I dug deeper and the story came out in bursts of emotional distraction. There were no tears yet, but I felt it was just a matter of time. And to think I had believed in the beginning of our business relationship that I could provide the services for her down-to-earth wedding without any emotional outbursts – who was I kidding? She shed some more light on the situation.

"His camera, the photographer's TOP NOTCH camera," I sensed a trace of sarcasm, "had a fault and now we have no photos. Not one picture from him. Remember all that stuff at the house, too? All for nothing, nada!"

Occasionally - just occasionally - I wished I had kept some strong alcohol at the salon. The best I could do was offer a cup of tea but she declined. I stretched my memory to six weeks before and the wedding....

"Your photographer was John Fielding, right?"

"Right."

John Fielding…I knew his work and that he was a good photographer with a reputation for reliability, too. Reliability in the sense of showing up on the day and promptly delivering the goods post wedding - and well before the couple's first anniversary. He could be very artistic with a camera, although his tools had let him down on this particular job and that was sad, indeed. Naturally, I was personally annoyed for Charlene, but professionally, I also cringed to think of this poor man's dilemma. Charlene obviously did not share my empathy.

"I need you to come in on this. Other than some hokey snapshots from friends we have no pictures of the wedding. No, no wedding album AT ALL."

Her eyes were red and glistening with a mélange of reluctant tears and anger. Then came the stinger.

"So we're going to do a repeat."

A repeat? This from the girl who could barely tolerate any fuss the first time? Life was strange. Very strange, indeed.

"No photos of your big day?" I murmured this to myself almost in disbelief. This had never happened before to any wedding I was involved in but I had heard that such a situation – again, as old wives' tales go – a very bad omen for the marriage, per se. I was reluctant to share the thought with Charlene who was in enough pain already. We had all mocked the 'weddings and green should never be seen' comment. Maybe we should have taken more notice.

"Right, Charlene." I decided it was time to be professional and organized, "Which services will you require exactly?"

She explained how the nuptials would be redone. The Wedding Part Two would transpire in a way that would involve re-hiring all of the outfits, dresses and kilts – just for a photo shoot. The fresh bouquets would have to be reproduced again too. Also on the list would be a three-tier cake and limos. What a rigmarole…

"No guests, not even grandparents," she winced at that one. "I asked them but Gran and Grandpa Currie are away back down to Gloucester where they live and my other grandparents have a trip abroad booked so they said go ahead without them. I think they're too knackered to do it again, anyway. So there you go. It can never be quite the same as the original, right? No matter how hard you try."

Did I detect a hint of regret, of sentimentalism?

She spread out her very tanned long arms for effect. "We're having just a park location near here, at Northend Park and a little shoot at the Viking Hotel again. So we will need a cake for that, too. The management at the Viking have been understanding about the situation. Of course, they know the photographer through business so that probably helps." She paused reflectively. "The staff there told me this has never happened before to their customers. And they were shocked that it DID happen to our Mr. Fielding, the ace photographer..."

She threw back her long copper tresses agitatedly.

"Tell me, is all this possible for you? He wants to get it done next week, a Tuesday. Of course it means that Callum and I will have to brown nose another day off work – after six weeks absence already!"

I looked at the diary. Hired dresses for a last-minute midweek sounded like a bonus business thing for me but the opposite was true. My hire stock would be tied up over two weekends because of cleaning and possible alterations. But it was fine. The gowns had not been out since Charlene's photo-jinxed date and were totally available. They were already cleaned and ready to go, alterations still intact. Big relief. I had to warn her that not everything would be so straightforward.

"I'll phone the baker straightaway for another cake but I can tell you it will be all sponge, no time for rich fruit."

Charlene stepped back into the former hard-headed version of herself for a moment.

"It can be a cardboard cake for all I care, so long as it looks similar to the original. Less fattening, too! The main thing is making everything look good and…authentic. That's it, basically. Fake, but good!"

"So do I send the invoice for all this to you?" I said, feigning innocence while knowing for certain the unlucky snapper would be coughing up. I was right.

"Send it to John Fielding, the so-called photographer…" She looked a little miffed.

"I shouldn't be too harsh because he has been pretty good about all this. He's definitely not side-stepping his responsibilities. He's offered to pay for all the props. Make out your bill and send it right away so you can be paid beforehand."

My silent-movie look of surprise must have been just too obvious.

"He wants you to do that, he told me so."

Poor old John Fielding having to stump up for the second act of this wedding. His was not a large business so I hoped he had good liability insurance to cover the expenses on the replay. I said as much to Charlene.

"I know. You're right. But at least we're trying to hold it down a little." She was racking her brain. "And did I mention the cars? Well, in fact we need just one limo, not three like we had on the day, remember? Callum and I can be in the Rolls to get to the park and hotel. That will do since it's just for photos. Everyone else will go in their own personal cars." She started to take on an apologetic stance. "Nobody wants to get dolled up and do this again, you know. Neil, the best man, was supposed to go white water rafting up north but he's postponed it for a few days. Gosh, you should have heard him about all of this. He's so-oo-oo mad! No wonder!"

"How about your make-up artist and hairdressers? All part of the big picture, right?"

"Yep. Fielding is taking care of that, too. They'll all be at the house Tuesday morning. Oh, the house! I told him no photos at the house. I'm not going through that again. Not bloody likely!"

I smiled in agreement. I was amazed she had tolerated it the first time.

She turned to me as she left the salon and, for the first time in our meeting, smiled. She was probably very relieved that my wedding paramedics would be on their way.

"Talking about the house, remember to have us picked up from OUR new home…not my mum's, this time!" I took note of the address again, just to be sure. The second time around needed no errors.

Everything was ready for the following week. There would be no problems or snags at my end since the clients had already taken their hire gear by the Saturday. The Rolls Royce was polished and ready to rumble and I had seen to it that the cake was safely positioned at the Viking.

All that was left was for me to personally trek round in the van with the fresh bouquets on the day itself, only this time to the newly wed couple's brand new villa designed for the two of them, by the two of them. It was mid morning as I drove the van into their circular driveway. I admired their choice of an ultra-modern designed home, totally befitting the personality of the bride, at least. I had not got to know the groom well prior to the original wedding, which was not an unusual situation. Brides were more my thing. I always said that the girls organized and the guys

229

showed up and Charlene's no-nonsense wedding, by its very nature, double emphasized this point. And if I had had little opportunity to become acquainted with the groom's personality before, then there was almost no chance of checking him out now. But as I went into the large, open plan living room carefully balancing the bouquets of sweet-smelling freesia and roses, I had a notion that it could be possible to find out how he was with all this retake business.

That was because Callum was with the female wedding cast this time. But any thoughts of getting a chat with this second-time-around groomie soon disappeared. I had been to hundreds of brides' family homes at this point in my career but never to one where a groom was right there in the middle of the girly inaction – spread out on the sofa looking unfazed and relaxed and absolutely not at all ready to do female chat. It was no shock to discover that he was pretty unexcited by the 'wedding part two' scenario. He looked quite bored and was more interested in watching re-runs of tennis grand slams on television. Of course it was unnatural for him to be there at all, ordinarily.

It really hit me for the first time that the excitement of the real wedding day just could not be regenerated, even with the girls. Since today's 'wedding' was merely a performance it occurred to me that I had been taking lots of things for granted. The ladies were not at all buzzing with energy – it was as if someone had burst the balloon, let all the air out. It was just a mockup, a play, a piece of theatre. So were all the actors script-perfect? Surely everyone knew their parts in this mini-fiasco, having already enacted them only weeks before? I asked anyway, and was assured that all was well.

"Of course we'll be just fine," said Charlene, yawning over a luscious smelling Costa coffee a caring bridesmaid had fetched. "There's no church, no congregation. Not a lot of time limits." Big yawn. "It's just a photo-shoot, really. It'll be a dawdle." Huge yawn. "The hair and makeup people will be here soon. I mean, come on, what can possibly go wrong?" Comatose yawn….

"Of course you're right, Charlene. We've already been down that road. We've used up all the jokers in the pack of cards, yeah?" Sandra, the chief bridesmaid got her sardonic tuppence in.

We all laughed. With all the fuss I had forgotten to ask Charlene a vital question when she had come running to the salon the week before. Now there was time and space for relaxed chat. That is, if no one actually fell asleep.

"How did that exotic six week honeymoon go? Did you both manage okay with the scuba diving?"

Finally, wake up time. Her face seemed to light up and glow. But perhaps it was just the effects of the expensive coffee. Who knows?

"Oh, our honeymoon in Thailand! It was heaven on earth. And we're now expert scuba-divers, really expert. Right, Callum?"

Callum's eyes did not leave the television screen. He simply grunted. I believe if she had told him his personally designed house was on fire he still would have simply grunted. Charlene however, looked quite wistful for a moment, obviously mulling over the nirvana that was Thailand. I had never seen that look on her lovely face when she was working with me on her first wedding, let alone the second. But Thailand – that was a different thing altogether….

"Oh my goodness! Oh, I never told you about it? It was a honeymoon and a half, honestly! I just wish we could both have a repeat shot at that. Eh, Callum?" It seemed her words fell on her new husband's deaf, tellytitis ears. It was possible his hearing had been affected by scuba diving and the depths of the warm salt Thai water. In search of an attentive audience, Charlene turned her attention exclusively to me.

"You know….I would love to have another chance to retake the honeymoon, yes indeed. To experience a special trip one more time - I wouldn't mind repeating Thailand, not one little bit. But life never happens like that, does it?"

My poor ears sadly had not had the opportunity to be affected by the warm South China Seas. Therefore, unlike her beloved, I managed to hear Charlene loud and clear.

"No," I said. "Not very often. No."

The Fiery Wedding

"Who presents this woman to be….."

Dring…dring….dring….dring….

The middle-aged Justice of the Peace conducting the civil ceremony looked irritated as he was forced to take his attention away from his humdrum ritual - and the confused bride and groom.

Mr. Swanson stood straight up to his full height of five feet three and nervously addressed the four dozen or so perplexed-looking guests in this small, fragrant, flower embellished marriage room. He adjusted his spectacles frantically, as if this exercise would help to turbocharge him, in the absence of a microphone, to yell at the top of his voice and be heard above the screeching, relentless, brain-penetrating, ringing din now invading the calm serenity of his workplace. It was obvious that this gentleman was a creature of habit and normality and the fire alarm had no place in his order of things. The proof of his displeasure was evident in his angry, flustered yell.

"Ladies and gentlemen, of course that is a fire alarm you are hearing. Everyone has to leave the building immediately. Take your belongings and then please follow me to the exits downstairs."

He hastily tidied the paperwork lying on the small desk behind him, popped everything into an official looking cardboard file holder, and with a miffed expression, headed for the door. I noticed the bride and groom Leanna and Tom holding each other nervously and looking around in panic at the sudden unexpected chaos. In seconds Leanne seemed to recover enough to retrieve her dignity and her dropped bouquet from the thick blue rug under her satin-clad feet and started off for the way out, hanging onto her almost-but-not-quite husband. Since I was already seated at the back of the room next to the exit, I jumped up quickly and was first to follow our snappish registrar, tailgating him out to and all the way along a brightly lit corridor to the already busy emergency stairs.

The hordes of employees of this huge government building had certainly lost no time in responding to the alarm, no matter how unfriendly the sound. Surprisingly, the general impression from their body language and chatter as we descended was not one of panic. Instead the unflappable mob moved rhythmically and orderly, generally in pairs, like the animals boarding Noah's Ark. I had a sneaky feeling that this huge work force had experienced this little exercise before. Two congested flights later we hit solid ground and made our way out to the massive car park crowded with more people than vehicles. Hundreds of members of staff still seemed to be oozing out of every pore of the huge, modern, austere and ugly concrete building, the Caledonia Centre. I suddenly agonized that if I didn't round up my little wedding party straightaway we could all get lost in the massive melee of humanity. No, they should be easy enough to find, I reassured myself. There was one easy way to spot them – everyone was dressed for a wedding with lots of hats and kilts– not to mention a bride with a big white ganache of a gown. That did make things a little simpler, for sure.

This was one for the books. I had done countless weddings at this stage of my career but had been lucky enough never to be ousted out of a ceremony by fire – or at least a fire alarm. I looked around for everyone – weren't Leanne and Tom down yet? Guilty thoughts of my scurrying down those stairs for my own for self-preservation began to surface. I should have ensured that Leanne was safely managing her dress and veil in such a situation where moving speedily was not an easy option. And I called myself a wedding planner! Imagine, I had just abandoned my clients, allowing them to be possibly barbecued at their own wedding. Oh, my….

I looked across the car park to our two Mercedes and Jaguar and saw my two chauffeurs Gally (short for Gallagher) and Archie loyally standing beside our wedding vehicles, parked neatly against a huge wall. This was routine, but just now it appeared that the drivers were intent on guarding them from the ever-increasing, madding crowd. They would be wondering, as I was, what on earth was to happen now, but both men stood still and unruffled, like the guards at Buckingham Palace. The two uniformed drivers had opted to stay with the cars whilst I went into the marriage room – a very long fifteen minutes ago - with my clients, whom I now seemed to have mislaid.

I finally spied the loving couple huddled together with their bridesmaids and best man – all of them looking uncomfortable and cold and anxious. It was a bitter February afternoon and having everyone thrown outside into the cruel, windy elements was not what I had anticipated. I could handle the ebb and flow of any wedding - goodness knows I had managed enough of them - but I had no control over some things. In this case, bad weather and unwanted fire alarms.

No! There was something I could do about the cold, at least. Thinking that this whole setup would likely be a very brief false alarm I thought better of schlepping the whole wedding party across the mammoth car park towards our big, comfy cars. It would only be a few minutes or so till we went back in…. hardly worth bothering folk, but meantime…..I set off towards the limos and my two knights in shining uniform.

"Let's bring the wee blankets out of the boots of the cars, lads."

I had made these little cozy fleece wraps myself for the bad weather days – nasty days. But not always nasty enough for some ambitious, tunnel-visioned photographer to abandon their artistic dreams of creativity and stop subjecting clients to cold, wind and even rain. It was those warm wraps which hit the spot under such circumstances.

"Aye, it's good we have these in the cars for the customers," said Archie, who liked to have a wee moan on occasions. "And I'm gonna put on my big overcoat to keep me warm an' all. It's bloomin' Baltic oot here. Ah, here it is in the boot."

Gally joined him by donning his own overcoat and commented wryly, "Archie. Wi' these big coats and the peaked caps we look like a couple o' penguins. In a wee minute the folk'll be chucking raw fish to us, mark my words."

"Raw fish? Dinna' fancy that. But a fish supper would go down a treat, absolutely."

Both drivers scooped up a dozen little shawls and took them over to our group who were happy to throw them round their shoulders. The males gallantly declined and conceded to the bride, her maids and other female guests, all of them scantily dressed, February or no February. As I looked on at their cute, dainty chiffon and silk flimsy dresses and two-pieces, it was definitely not up for debate that when it came to putting style first, sometimes we women could be stark raving bonkers. Many of the lads were intelligently sporting heavy worsted wool Bonnie Prince Charlie jackets - with waistcoats, to boot. The kilts themselves were cozy, too, if a little draughty underneath. But perhaps they were wearing heavy thermal underwear – or as rumoured, no underwear at all? Never! Well, not in mid-winter anyhow.

Leanne was not really as horrified at the whole fire alarm incident as I had expected. She, like her guests, had decided to be optimistic. When I asked her how she was bearing up she smiled and squared up the sparkly tiara framing her upswept dark, thick hair. I was glad she had chosen a long-sleeved dress from the salon. Much less chance of goosebumps.

"I think we'll be back inside in a few minutes," she smiled. "Probably a false alarm, but it's always something to tell our grandchildren about, right?"

Her other half decided to play droll devil's advocate. Tom was a strapping fair-haired six-footer and squatted a little to be level to his bride's pretty face.

"Leanne, Leanne…maybe we should start with telling our future CHILDREN first. Leave the grandweans out of this. I can't think that far ahead, darlin'." He thought for a few seconds then added, "Although I have to say I've sprouted a few old man grey hairs in the last few minutes – aye, I have."

He pulled a shock horror face making everybody laugh as they blew into their hands to keep warm. Our bride still seemed upbeat a minute or so later as she snuggled into Tom's shoulder and he put his long arms right around her. They were both dealing with it well, in spite of the two shiny red fire engines now whizzing into the zone. Inevitably we were all ordered to retreat well away from the building for safety. I was taking the situation a bit more seriously now, for if it was a false alarm I wondered why they still had to have the emergency services on the scene. The wedding party started to voice more serious concern, too. Was this wedding to take place today or not?

The fire team set about their business lickety-split as a half dozen strong men charged inside. Surely we would get things sorted out quickly now, I hoped. After all, the cavalry had shown up. They would simply hose things down, if there even WAS a fire and then normal wedding life could resume. I enjoy happy endings, but life is not always like that.

The employees in the car park were becoming a little restless, too. I have never been averse to absorbing the opinions of others and with so much of the workforce nearby this was prime time for finding out how normal or abnormal this type of thing happened. Politicians and wedding planners have to remember that one must listen to the voice of the man and woman in the street. So I did. Had they experienced this type of thing often - perhaps they knew the ropes, fire-wise? One pair of ladies beside me were more than willing to share their forceful, loud opinions.

"I thought this would be a false alarm again, didn't I, Alana? We had one last month, remember? But now I'm no' so sure. Bringin' in the fire brigade, now that's serious. If I'd thought for a minute it was a real fire I would've grabbed that smashin' Michael Kors bag Kyle gave me for Christmas. That beautiful handbag cost a fortune and it could get ruined. Who says there isn't a bonfire going on up there? We would normally be back at our desks by now if the alarm wasnae' genuine."

Her friend drew her own conclusions.

"I think you're right as usual, Tamara." She then addressed me. "But I'll tell ye. Ye must know I feel sorry for this wee wedding today, but could they not just please let everyone get a bit closer to this blinkin' fire, if there is one. I could fair do with a wee bit of heat right now...."

Tamara was not finished on the subject of fire safety protocol. "Why do they always tell ye' to

242

leave everything and get out? Bampots. It's bloody freezing out here. And to think I'm only worried about my designer handbag. I wished I'd grabbed my Ted Baker cashmere and wool coat, an' all."

Her face took on a dreamy, if slightly smug expression. "That was another wee present. Remember I told ye about it, Alana? Aye, Kyle bought that for me, as well – from Harvey Nichols. For Valentine's Day. That man is so good to me, so good to me." She turned to me solicitously.

"Ah hope your bride has a man that good…."

These savvy women were more sure than not that there was a real live fire performing inside. But I kept my fingers crossed that it was just fake news and that it would not take too long to get us back into the nuptial fray. My runner-up wish was that maybe it would just be a tiny wee fire. With just a slight whiff of smoke. I was reassured by the memory of my nuisance smoke alarm at home which was so sensitive the family was nervous making toast. It over reacted and sounded at the merest hint of heat so I was always having a moan at Other Half to dissemble it and he always calmly refused me. Bloody nuisance. The smoke alarm, I mean.

Since the clients' wedding had barely kicked off when the bells sounded we still had a whole ceremony to finish, hopefully. The time was now almost twenty-five past two. I made a decision and marched over to the wedding cars where Archie and Gally were still waiting coldly and patiently.

"Let's get the main party into the cars. Even with the blankets it's still brass monkeys."

I had assumed people would comply and they did. It was practically a stampede to get to the limos and warmth. Happy to shelter, Leanne and Tom slid along the slinky beige leather of the Jaguar's rear seat and the best man jumped in front. The others shared the two Mercedes comfortably – the bridesmaids in their chic midnight blue shantung gowns and four parents with a granny. As poor grandma climbed in she was bitterly complaining about her life possibly being in danger. She had started to feel a potential resurge of a recent bout of pneumonia.

"Aye, there's something to be said for a June wedding, right enough," said Granny. "I've been not well since the New Year when I had threatened pneumonia," she explained.

I speculated silently that since it was merely 'threatened' it had never actually materialized.

However, Granny was sticking to her pulmonary guns.

"I've not been the same since. It's not easy when you're eighty years old, getting over life-threatening illnesses."

Tom decided to pull her leg.

"Gran, is that right? Are you eighty, right enough? I would never have thought that." At this, Granny brightened up slightly. Then he went on, peering into her face studiedly.

"You know Gran, I hiv to say this… you don't look a day over seventy-nine!"

More laughter from our appreciative, if chilled audience. This was a good crowd, full of banter. And boy, oh boy, did we need banter….but I had to get serious.

"We'll try to get some more info on the fire situation. For now all the car engines are running for heat," I told the bridal couple. "And the drivers are on call outside, see?"

Archie and Gally were holding up well, thanks to their 'penguin suits' – the heavy navy-blue wool overcoats, hats and thick leather gloves.

"Are you both ok, gentlemen?" I asked the two stalwarts. "You could always join the young people's parties inside the limos, remember. If you're really cold."

"Well, it's no' exactly June, but whit can we do?" Gally muttered through chattering teeth. "I wish I had brought my flask wi' me. I could have had a hot cuppa tea."

Archie had different priorities. "And we canna' smoke inside the cars, either. Whit a choice, eh?"

I nodded exaggeratedly. Smoking - and I did so myself in those early days - was taboo inside wedding limos.

I pulled up my own trouser suit jacket collar, ready to set back to the hub for more info. The realization that time was rolling on hit me when a gleaming large white executive coach purred past me, then parked up tidily alongside our wedding vehicles. It was the wedding guest coach and had been due to arrive as the wedding was finishing. I had ordered this fifty-seater executive vehicle as part of the plans and here it was, shiny and polished and ready to transport its load of post-wedding guests straight to the reception. Ready to journey them to the delightfully cozy hotel reception venue where heart-warming cocktails, champagne and canapes would await them on silver trays. I was sure the shivering guests would have been delighted to take off to this happy, drinky-snacky land, namely the Regent Hotel, a mere, blissful fifteen minutes away from here. Only one problem – the wedding had not even started yet, let alone finished.

Sure enough, the wedding guests were almost drooling at the vision of the white coach, their passport to warmth and comfort. When I briefed the stout, uniformed driver he was unsure about what to do next.

I liked my team to be rigid about schedules. That was vital, but this officious fellow was annoying. He rolled back on his heels and reminded me: "I showed up at half-past two as scheduled and I'm supposed to drop off at the Regent at quarter-past three latest. I can't hold on any longer than that, 'cos I've got other jobs." His overt confidence seemed to forsake him for a few seconds. "I'm no' sure whit to do here."

He was a new driver, one I did not recognize from Cameron Coaches. I sympathized with him and everyone else stuck in this wedding from hell. But I had to remain assertive. There was a wedding at stake.

"I was just on my way to find out so you should be wiser in a few mins. Ok? But look, if the guests could sit it out in your coach in the meantime that would be great. They're all crumbling with cold and we don't want to kill the customers now, do we?"

I tried to sound confident but deep down there were gigantic butterflies partying inside my rumbly tummy. I attributed this sensation to the uncertainty of it all because military precision was normally our mantra. The wedding guests were ushered into the coach. If not disgruntled, they certainly were not gruntled.

"I thought I wis goin' to a weddin' the day, no' a charabanc," one grumpy gentleman threw at me as he boarded the bus.

His wife apologized for him. "It's no' your fault, hen. We know that. Don't listen tae him."

She then sought my professional advice as she collapsed, in relief, into a thickly padded luxury velvet coach seat.

"Do ye think if I take off these new high heels I'll be able to get them back on again? My feet are absolutely killin' me, so they are. Ah wish I'd brought a spare pair."

I nodded. I hoped she would not define the nod as an answer to the shoe removal question. It was more a nod of acquiescence to the great wisdom of hauling along a more familiar, spare pair. Magnificent words of advice for anyone about to explore the glamorous, excruciatingly painful world of untried very high heels. Especially at an all-day wedding.

With all the goings-on I still hadn't checked the fire situation. I popped my head into the couple's Jag again to keep them posted that I hadn't forgotten and that the guests were now toasty-warm in the coach. Amazingly, no one seemed to be panicking. I soon found out why.

"Don't worry about us – we're all okay," Tom assured me, sounding unnaturally un-nervous.

"See this," he pulled a sizeable silver whisky flask from his lap and shook it, inches from my face. The weak swish told me there was some fragrant amber liquid left in it, but not much.

"We've all had a nice wee dram and we're about to start on Gary's flask now. Ha, ha, ha!"

The best man Gary turned round to smile crookedly. He was opening his kilt sporran as he spoke to his pal.

"Here it is, Tom. Vive la flask, eh?"

Tom kept me posted. "Don't worry about us. We're no' crying yet, although the bad news is my flask is nearly empty. But the good news is...."

He leaned right across Leanne's voluptuous chiffon skirts till he was inches from my face at the car window. The intoxicating power of his breath made me start to feel tipsy, too.

"Do you know what the good news is, eh? Well, the good news is Gary's flask is a really big one. Aye, it's full to the gunwhales and it holds a lot more than mine, eh, Gary? Thank goodness you've got a great big sporran, too. Ha, ha, ha!"

Leanne did not appear to be tiddly but her cheeks had certainly acquired a rosier hue than before. Oh, well, I thought. Good luck to them. The whole thing was ridiculous anyway.

 I went off, soberly, to find out if Rome was actually burning or were we all being fiddled, or diddled, perhaps.

It had not been established if there were other couples waiting to be married after Tom and Leanne's wedding. Somehow I didn't think so, as civil registry ceremonies usually kept a tight schedule with weddings practically every hour on the hour. In fact, some establishments allowed only forty-five minutes between, which I had always thought very tight. Our affair had been booked for two o'clock which would likely be the last of that day's schedule. Four o'clock was closing time, especially on a Friday. However, it was quite possible.....

Sure enough, two beautiful, gleaming burgundy limos appeared in the already over-crowded human parking area. What a circus this was turning out to be. They parked well away from the biz and eventually one of the chauffeurs, very tall, liveried and handsome, sauntered over to me and my own motley crew of drivers. He was keen to know what was happening.

"We've had a bit of a hold-up with our wedding here today," I said to him. "Are you going to join the wedding queue with your clients or are you just window shopping?" I sounded like a real smart-ass, but all this stuff was really getting to me. Besides, as elegant as he was, he annoyingly flaunted a crumbly, extra-large sausage roll partly clothed in its original bakery shop paper bag and nibbled on it tauntingly. Unashamedly. For all of us peckish people to see. I wished I had brought snacks. The timing of this wedding discounted lunch altogether for everyone concerned, plus the brisk, cold air really pumped up the appetite. I could have murdered a cup of tea and a ham sandwich, at least…

The Greek God chauffeur attempted to assuage my curiosity. With his sausage-roll-free large hand he wiped a flaky crumb from his sculpted cheek. "No, our wedding was already at twelve o'clock here," he told our envious assembly. "All done and dusted. We've just dropped the whole party off at the reception in Whitburn after the usual photo trip, of course," he said, rolling his rather nice bright blue eyes.

"Trouble is, I was given a very generous tip to get back here for the bride's gran's handbag. Left it in the marriage room upstairs, would you believe."

"Well, if there is a fire, the bag could have turned into a well done hamburger by now," said Archie. "We don't know whit's happening and they won't let you into the building. Shame about that tip – the refundable one, I mean."

"Archie! Behave yourself!" I said, detecting a hint of jealousy. Was this because of the succulent sausage roll or reference to the tip? Talk of tips tended to rouse emotion amongst wedding chauffeurs. Most of them saw tips as financial bonuses but others recognized them as symbols of hierarchy, like winning a BAFTA. I

252

knew from experience that Archie was the BAFTA type. The suave chauffeur seemed to be immune to the green bullets of envy fired at him. He remained cool and collected, above such pettiness.

"Oh, well. When I get back home I'll phone the hotel reception and tell them about poor old Granny's handbag. I'll just head off then after I tell my mate Jim it's no go. He pulled in with me when he saw the fire brigade. He could have headed back to the garage in Shettleston but he was desperate to know the score. Nosey bugger is Jim. Oh, well, I'll be glad to get back home on a nippy day like this, anyway. Nice hot plate o' homemade soup waiting for me, eh? Cheers."

We all looked on wistfully as he strolled off, still annoyingly clutching his tasty sausage roll, back to his enticingly warm car and his curious mate Jim. In an hour or less they would have dropped off their limos at their base in the east end of Glasgow and then be home to a warm meal. To central heating and telly. We all sighed - but glared at the same time. Jealousy is an odious thing.

I was being distracted at every turn but finally I took the bull by the horns and storm trooped towards one of the fire engines to catch someone in the know. Besides, storm trooping got the blood circulating.

A very young, vague fire fighter sporting a name badge labelled 'Troy', was alone inside one of the engines. I appealed to him but he could not help me at all. He impassively put down his copy of the Sun and placed his packet of cheese and onion crisps carefully and resignedly on the empty seat beside him as he turned reluctantly to me, the pest who had disturbed him. I gazed greedily at his crisps. I loved cheese and onion. But not quite as much as sour cream and chives. They were excellent. And you could make a nice crisp butty with them, especially with crusty bread. And a hot cup of tea, too. That really made it.

I pulled myself together and tried to focus on his reply, his pearls of wisdom.

"I'm supposed to be observing today," he informed me politely. I refrained from reminding him his red top journal was blocking his view. "I'm in training so I don't really do the hands-on fire stuff like the others. If I see Tommy – my boss - I'll try and find out for you what's going on. Okay?" His patience had obviously been fully spent. With this, he picked up his tabloid and his crisps and resumed his pleasant life of non-firefighting, non-observance and nonchalance.

Assuring him I would be eternally grateful to him and Tommy, I hung around for a minute or so in the cruel cold next to the fire engine, kind of like a groupie at a pop concert. Perhaps it was the colour red that made me feel a bit warmer. Subconsciously. Psychosomatically. Like those images people put up on their television in winter showing a film of thriving hot coals in a fireside. Apparently it caused sweat glands to react and some folk even had to strip off, such was the suggestion of cozy heat. Oh, well. I hoped the fire engine would do that for me, but so far it was definitely not working.

I wasn't even supposed to be here today. Since the salon was fairly quiet I had decided to chauffeur the Jag which was my favourite car of all. I adored the polished walnut dash, the sweet, rich fragrance of the beige leather interior and the smoothness of the ride. The stereo system was fantastic, too. The fact that it needed two large fuel tanks and passed everything except a petrol station did not bother me. It was a car to love. Besides, as the wedding planner, today I could make sure my bridal couple got a good sendoff into supposedly marital bliss. I had not

255

anticipated the struggle to launch them into any marital state, blissful or otherwise.

My unflinching mantra was 'if there is any trouble, I want to deal with it first hand'. I concluded that it was just as well I had come along to take charge – but was I taking charge? I was as much a victim as anyone else here and was powerless to do anything to change the circumstances. I could only keep people calm and comfortable – but time was running out fast. At last something was happening at the emergency exit door. People suddenly started to appear – a firefighter who was perhaps the esteemed Tommy, a security guard, and a trio of grey-haired, grey-suited, grey shod gentlemen who looked as if they were about to address the throng. Sure enough, one of them did. Archie and Gally had arrived at my side to hear the hopefully good news.

Cough, cough. "We apologise for the – erm - inconvenience you have all experienced here today. The underlying – eeh - problem was an - erm-electrical breakdown and fire which is now under control, but is still flawed enough to offend our –erm -Health and Safety regulations. However, all staff will now be free to enter the - er - building quickly and collect their- eh- belongings before leaving for the day. Members of the – eh, the - eh fire team will escort you to your various departments."

Oh, drat!

He went on to reveal our worst nightmare. Well, Tom and Leanne's worst nightmare.

"Since the building is not considered – eh - safe for working purposes, the wedding which was in progress at two o'clock will sadly have to be, erm…. erm…cancelled. Mr. Swanson here will- eh- speak to the wedding party in a moment…."

He babbled on about Health and Safety but I heard very little since my ears had either frozen over or closed down in disgust. My two sturdy chauffeurs prised them open again.

"No wedding! My God! And what about the reception? You can't have a reception without a wedding first – can you?" He turned to me looking quite desperate for answers. I had none. Gally was confused and he was not alone.

"Ye're kiddin'? After all this waitin' aboot we haven't got a wedding after all," from Archie, stating the bleeding obvious. "Whit now?"

"We'll soon find out. There's our Mr. Swanson headed over to speak to the couple now. I think we have a right to know what's going down here."

Like the Three Musketeers, we marched dutifully back to the cars, behind the short, balding, but powerful Mr Swanson.

The three of us stood back a little as the registrar spoke to the couple through the open car window.

"Hello, I am Samuel Swanson. You'll remember I started to officiate at your wedding. Sorry to tell you that there's no possibility of proceeding with the wedding today."

"Health and Safety, insurance and all the rest simply forbid it. I'm sorry."

Tom's previous flirtation with the whisky flask was immediately erased. He sounded much more sober than earlier. "What are you suggesting we do about actually getting married then Mr. Swanson? Eventually?"

Leanne said nothing. She showed emotion through the large teardrops now running down her perfectly made-up, charming face. Post hoc she put in a word, but her voice was almost a whisper.

"I can't believe this is happening. My family is here to see us get married and now it's cancelled?"

Poor Leanne, this was her worst nightmare. But I felt for old Swanson, too. I didn't envy his position as Satan's messenger.

"A team will work on it over the weekend. By Monday latest it will be sorted. And there will be financial compensations, too. You could come back Monday. I'm very sorry. Really. Here's my card. Call me tomorrow, no matter that it's Saturday. I'll deal with it all for you."

He turned on his smart, grey-brogued heel and started to head back to his work mates. I couldn't believe what I had just heard. Shocked, I took off to pin down the pin-striped civil servant. I asked him if there could be another way of dealing with this ridiculous scenario.

"Not really. Our office is closed so what CAN we do?"

I threw out an idea. "The Regent Hotel is only fifteen or twenty minutes away. Why can't you just go marry the couple over there?"

Swanson looked a bit non-plussed. "Well…their reception will not be set up for such an occasion. Usually these services are pre-prepared by the hotel staff etcetera."

"A minor point at such a moment, Mr. Swanson. This couple would consent to being married in the hotel kitchen, if needs be. But you know that won't happen. It would only take a few minutes in the hotel banquet area. The guests could take their normal dining places while you conduct the service and then the whole family could just get on with the celebrations. The options are not good – not good at all, as you already know."

Swanson knew there was nowhere else to go with this problem. He recognized it was the least he could do considering the situation. What was disappointing was his reluctance to save the day – at first.

He sighed wearily and relented. "Yes, I'll go to the Regent. I'll clear it with my people inside, if there is anyone inside, plus I need my files. Then I"ll come back and let you all know for sure. But it should be fine." He looked at his silver watch. "If we clear it, I could probably be over there in a half hour or less, ok?"

Tom had my admiration and respect as he spoke to his bride. I caught his words as I approached the Jaguar with the good news.

"Look, darling. So we don't have the piece of paper yet, but we're still starting the rest of our lives together right now, service or no service.

Our reception is waiting, so why don't we get going and enjoy that. There's no point in totally ruining our day, right? He took her damp little face in his big hands and kissed her very gently. "You know, if they handed me a dozen marriage certificates I couldn't love you more."

It was almost painful for me to interrupt such a pretty speech but I knew the news was too important.

They were over the moon.

Tom bolstered Leanne again about their topsy-turvy wedding day.

"Leanne, it'll be fine. We're meant to get married today. Remember, you were talking about stories to tell the grandweans about the alarm – well now it's an even better story. You definitely couldna' whack this one!"

The bride sat up straight and wiped her face with a Handy Andy. I had popped my own personal packet in through the car window.

"Okay," she smiled, a little weakly. "We'll get right over to the reception. And maybe for the sake of our kids and grandkids, I'll marry you while I'm over there."

She continued with her own little leg pull.

"But I'll have to see how I feel…."

Phone Calls

The phone call was short and to the point. "Hello, this is Paula Burns' sister, Julie. I'm calling to tell you that the wedding in three weeks will have to be cancelled."

"Oh, dear….why is that?

There was a breathy, ten second pause.

"Paula died. Thank you."

Then she hung up.

I stood for a few seconds – maybe it was five minutes - with the phone still in my hand, staring at it senselessly. Glaring at it, illogically. Sometimes this phone delivered wonderful, happy things to my world - but today it was an enemy, a bearer of terrible news.

She died....

"What happened?" I whispered to the buzzing, defunct receiver. "Was it an accident, was she ill?"

She had been to see us just the other week and looked fine. We had caught up with her final fittings which were unproblematic, meaning Paula had no need to chip in comments about this or that. She was a quiet girl by nature and tended to let the bridesmaids take over the occasion. I pondered at the time that she really didn't have to be there at all, since the girls were more than capable of handling their own fitting and ensuring we were not about to fob them off with excessively long or baggy gowns for the big day.

"I'm so happy," Julie couldn't stop smiling, just to prove the point. "I DID lose that six pounds and it shows." She turned to the bride and her other bridesmaid sister. "Can you see it - look? Margaret, you told me I hadn't lost an ounce...."

Meanwhile Paula wore a glimmer of a smile and silently let them get on with it.

It all seemed very petty now.

I was upset by the tragic news but asserted my business brain. There was work to be done, cancellations to be discussed. That's what the phone call was about, after all.

"We're cancelling. She died. She died…."

Because it was imminent, the Burns order was top of the pile of papers on our big, back shop office desk, so no hunting required there. I morosely and distractedly shuffled through copies of cake orders, drivers' sheets, flower lists, alteration invoices and the rest. We were at that time dabbling in computer files and of course I personally did not trust them. Good old rustling, crackling paper order forms for this cautious boss who was quite BC. I needed time to digest the horror of the moment, but the sickening, vindictive little phone would not let up. It beckoned me to seize it, and the moment, to let some of our team know the score. My first calls were to the baker, the photographer and videographer. It was painful, but also it was only fair to deal with this as early as possible.

She died?

"John? Yeah, it's me. Won't need the cake for the Burns wedding next week….Don't know exactly – a family tragedy, I hear. We're holding deposits but I can get back to you about all that in view of the situation. Right, John. Ok, talk to you soon. Bye."

She died.

"Hi, Jeff. Yeah, bridal shop here. Just heard the Burns wedding is off for Saturday, the 19th. This month, that's right. Sorry about all this. I know - of course you would have met with the couple last week to finalise the photo plans. No, I really don't know what happened for sure but there definitely is a genuine reason for cancelling. Got to get on it now, but I'll be sure to contact you again later. Ok. Right. Everything else is good for the other dates through till October. Yes. Bye, Jeff."

She really died…..

Driving home that evening I mentally floated back to the seven months before when Paula arrived to choose her dresses. As usual I made sure she knew about all our other services, tempting her into ordering more goodies and creating a larger bill. That was good business and I always encouraged my staff to employ this tactic.

"Let people know what we have on offer," I would remind them. "There's no need for a customer here to go anywhere else for services. Do them a favour and remind them we can cover all their needs - now remember…!"

Consequently Paula added a cake, photos, video and limousines to her order of two bridesmaid dresses and flowers. She had already chosen her wedding gown elsewhere which was a pity, I thought at the time. Not just for the extra business, but because it would have been great to garb her – with her neat little figure and short, thick bobbed dark hair. She was not naturally striking – but in the right dress, with all the trimmings, make-up and hair, she would have been quite stunning. It was always thrilling in this job to turn ordinary girls into princesses. I adored that part.

I saw her only twice after that initial meeting at the salon. The staff took care of the order and I was involved in minor ways only. One of the occasions was when my friend Carol, a college lecturer in Glasgow, had popped in to see me. Since I was busy with prep work she did not stay long but she did recognize Paula, a day release student at her college, discussing wedding plans with Marlon.

She approached the bride to say hello and they chatted briefly. Carol then told me that our girl Paula, a medical secretary, was an excellent part-time student, hardworking and attentive at her studies. This didn't surprise me at all since I had noted her calm way of dealing with her bridesmaids and her reactions to the other wedding plans we were coordinating for her. She absolutely would have been an efficient, capable student at Carol's secretarial classes. You just knew...

Paula was on my mind constantly after the eerie phone call and understandably it was disturbing for all of us in the salon to shrug off sadness, to deal coldly and systematically with creepy cancellation business and not think compassionately about the bride.

She died....

Of course we wondered what had really happened but since it was the middle of the season, for the first day or so we had to busy ourselves with the messy debris of this retraction. And we still had other weddings to focus on – other people's weddings.

We had the task of organizing the weddings of people who had not died.

A couple of days into the aftermath my unfriendly, unlikeable, frank little beige phone delivered one more dramatic message. It was my friend Carol telling me, too late, about Paula's demise.

"I know," I said. "I just don't know what happened. I couldn't ask the family. Not yet, anyway. Don't want to be too intrusive when they're all in pain. Do YOU know exactly what happened? Was it an accident?"

"No. It wasn't an accident. It's just tragic...."

"Oh, no. What then?"

The answer was horrific.

"She committed suicide."

Grab a Guy and Win a Free Wedding

When our all-inclusive wedding package was put onto the business menu it was an innovative move. No other company was providing a complete one-stop shop for couples – believe me, I checked.

I understand even Richard Branson, one of the globe's most successful entrepreneurs had a stab at it around the mid 90's and basically failed. The reason we succeeded was because we sold services under our personal control and if we sub-contracted help, it was through companies we knew and trusted. On my desk was the client's booking form, her bill and the buck. It all stopped there.

I truly believed in this product. It involved minimum hassle with free coordination thrown in, therefore by acquiring the package you were contracting all our services and they would be weaved together seamlessly to make the arrangements easier for you, your groom and also participating parents. Sure, there would always be those who loved to dash around from the dress shop to men's hire outfitters to bakers, photographers, limousine companies, florists and the rest. God bless them. Our clients would be teased that they did have to remember to arrange the church ceremony and the reception. And honestly, wasn't that enough to do? They would have three bills – from the church, the reception and us. Yes, there was plenty of stress to go around if you still wanted it, even with the package.

The all-inclusive wedding was so new in concept that we had to market it as aggressively as we could afford. Word of mouth was always our best reference although it was carrier pigeon slow. We also preached via radio, but mostly by newspaper advertising where I would often haggle for some extra free copy write-ups with the local paper. They did comply many times but I wanted more publicity for this new package. I knew that such an innovative concept would be a life-saver for many folk so I approached the local press with an idea for a competition, a "Win Your Dream Wedding" competition. We would provide all of our services to the winner absolutely free in exchange for many months of free advertising for our company and the all-inclusive package – all through their columns. They were excited at the idea. They would sell more newspapers since people had to buy and save cut-out coupons to apply. It would also create follow up interest and would stimulate extra wedding-related adverts for the newspaper, all from local companies with vested interests. The competition would be a winner for everyone, particularly the one lucky couple who would have a free wedding.

It was imperative that we stipulated the date for this wedding which had to be a midweek in low season – not a Saturday in August, for example, our prime time. A small compromise for a freebie, we thought. The competition was popular and went on for several months. There were tons of applicants who had to proclaim why they deserved to win the free wedding and we milked the publicity until finally the advertising chief who was in charge of the contest called to signal that the entry date had passed and it was time to choose the winners. Lana was that head of advertising for the paper and she arrived at the salon with a big leather briefcase full of hopeful entrants, photographs and all. God, it was amazing to see every one of the many, many applicants laid out pleadingly on my big white desk in the salon. I was starting to hear wedding bells ringing in my ears as we went through the lot of them.

"Aw, look at them, they seem like a lovely couple," Jinty voiced passionately. "Och, it would be nice to see them wed."

" Never mind those two, doesn't this girl have gorgeous long red hair, she would be a beautiful bride! And the fella looks like a real stud!" was Marlon's input, then followed by with the next photograph, "Oh, no. What a shame for this wee couple, they've been engaged for ten years, TEN years. They deserve to win it. Imagine being strung along for TEN years, that's just terrible, I think!"

This is how it went over two pots of tea and lots of M & S biccies, with the team, Lana and myself. Everyone was right into this. Jinty was in her element and I hadn't seen her so excited for years. Not since we had brought in the first full tulle Swan Lake ballerina dress. I looked at my watch – and my calendar. The chosen winning wedding would take place during the safe, quiet sanity of a lower season but right now – as we were fussing over the potential winners – it was high season and we had lots to do in the salon. I intimated we had to make a fast decision.

Certainly the contestants were potentially all winners, but there had to be some extra angle to it, some unusual aspect to set a couple aside, I insisted. Lana reminded us of one pair who had been engaged for only a year but had no hope of getting married for several years for financial reasons. Jinty dunked her chocolate digestive into her cuppa in sympathy and sighed wistfully while Lana continued.

"She's a local girl who met her fiancé up north at Dornoch in the highlands while she was visiting a family relative. They only see each other about once a month when he comes down here. They both live with their respective parents but of course they are dying to be together as a couple. What do you think?"

I thought it was a good choice. It was a romantic, lovelorn scenario as deserving as any other, so a decision was made. I agreed to give them the free wedding and release them from their heartbreaking detachment. By this time Jinty was shedding so many tears of emotion I began to wonder if she had spiked her own tea. When she recovered I put her in charge of first appointments for the couple, Kathy and Ken.

A couple of weeks after the newspaper announced the winners officially through their columns, the pair came into the salon, not overjoyed and bubbly as we had hoped, but shy and reticent. They say opposites attract but not in this case. Kathy and Ken seemed to be matched in nerves and apprehension as we took them through their free services. She fidgeted with her bag, opening and closing it as if she were testing the zip, nibbled on her already short fingernails on her left hand and twisted her fine, dark ash blonde hair into little ringlets with the other one. Ken seemed to be trying with his body language to reassure her by stroking her blue-jeaned kneecap or putting an arm around her thin shoulders – I wasn't sure if this was indeed for her benefit or his, for he himself wore the expression of a man about to go to the gallows. The two were extremely uncomfortable and it truly puzzled us. They were a very normal looking couple. He was tall and gangly with a ruddy complexion and light brown hair while she was very slim, petite and pale. I personally felt that under the circumstances their attitudes were disappointing. The staff felt it, too. Marlon was reaching for his little blue nerve pills.

"A wee smile would have been nice, no? I would have thought that a young couple who had just won a totally free wedding would have been overjoyed, not depressed. It's not as if we're even handing round the tip jar. I mean, come on!"

I went through the whole presentation of the package, their entitlements and the schedule we would need to establish in order to complete dress fittings for the bride and two bridesmaids as well as the men's fittings for tuxedos or kilts. They wished to have no changes to the free wedding – no extras whatsoever. I was a little surprised because the package was not set in stone and most brides changed things around a little, adding an extra bridesmaid or two or adding on another few male outfits. Not in this case, however.

To boot, before the winners had been announced in the paper, Lana had shrewdly cast her advertising net around the contest, snaring a few local companies. Some of these businesses, jewellers, travel agents, local hotels, confectioners all took advantage of the spotlight and a couple of them decided to jump feet first right into the matrimonial prize-giving. Suddenly the free wedding became even more free.

A local, fairly prestigious hotel threw in a reception for seventy people. Fabulous. Then a high street travel agent upped the prize to include a seven-day Majorcan honeymoon. Even more fabulous. The wedding rings were to be courtesy of our town's only jewellers. Was there anything left to worry about? It would seem there was nothing to sweat over, for Kathy and Ken would have it all free – lock, stock and bountiful barrel. We all expected joy and merriment. But every time they showed up at the salon for appointments we could just see misery. This was unnerving and puzzling for us - how could a couple who had just won a dream, free wedding not be over the proverbial moon about it? We all began to have doubts. Perhaps they had changed their minds about their engagement, the wedding, their future life together. The truth was that in spite of their gloomy postures they absolutely seemed to be in love. That was indisputable, so what was the problem....

Within a fortnight of our initial meeting the bride and her maids had chosen dresses and accessories. Kathy's choice of a white lace princess line gown with a short train suited her neat figure and personality, for it was unfussy and unostentatious. The bridesmaids were to be in peach satin, off the shoulder and it suited everyone that there were to be very few alterations. This was perfect, for I knew instinctively that Kathy did not want to be in the salon if she could help it. This was another enigma, for brides normally loved the buzz of our dress business, the choosing, the excitement of bridesmaids laughing together as they tried on good - and bad - selections. It normally involved good craic, good chick wit. Everyone had a jolly girls' day out including the staff – we would all be girls together in conspiratorial female fellowship. Even Marlon.

The groom's party was pretty straightforward with no troublesome fittings and were accommodated when they came down to Lanarkshire from the highlands. There was nothing unusual about this almost mundane routine, since the males involved in weddings were normally wholly different from their other halves. They didn't launch their own little giggle parties like the girls but instead would try on, be fitted and measured and then leave as quickly as possible, generally heading on to the pub. Ken's guys were no different other than we had to familiarize them, highlanders or not, with kilts and their paraphernalia such as sporrans (wee furry bags hanging from a chain belt) and the skean dhu (the dagger- filled sheath worn in the cuff of the long woolly socks) Experience had taught us that even for those who knew and adored the movie Braveheart, wearing the kilt for the first time could be a prickly, heather-covered mountainous challenge.

With the Royal Hotel coming into the picture and giving the free reception, I arranged to go see Tom Gallagher, the delightful owner and business associate of ours. It was vital that we both became familiar with the greater plan in order for

278

the big day to go smoothly. We knew how the other operated since we had worked together many times with weddings, wedding fayres and fashion shows so there was confidence on both sides. Tom filled me in with his arrangements. "The meal is for seventy people and they have stretched that to seventy-five. They are sticking to the basics so it's chicken for everyone and the minimum of wine on the table." He shrugged and looked at me as if he expected me to explain the apparent frugality but I had nothing to add other than we were experiencing the same situation at our end.

"Perhaps they just don't have any resources at all, perhaps they ARE truly deserving," was his quiet comment.

Perhaps he was right. We tidied up the schedule between us and confirmed again that we would do our best to make it a great day for the lucky couple, but what I had heard from the Royal owner compounded my own apprehensions. Were we digging a deep hole for this young pair? Sure, the wedding was basically free, but some extras of their own may have accumulated, a problem in a situation where there was a shortage of spare cash to cover those extras.

At the bride's final fitting, just two weeks before the day, some light was shed on the issue. Kathy was becoming more trusting and relaxed in our company obviously, because she started to open up a little. "I don't think I have thanked you for giving us this prize," she said as she stood shivering with nerves as usual and making it tough for poor Jinty to pin her. She was right. It was the first expression of gratitude from her. Not that we lusted after gratitude. Just happy, bubbling normal excitement.

"My parents can't help us much as they are retired now, and Ken's parents are a bit old-fashioned. They think it's not their place to chip in, so we are on our own financially and if it wasn't for this prize, we would have to wait years to get married."

So Tom Gallagher and I were right. Even with a free wedding this was a big stretch. It was sad, but I managed an understanding, upbeat posture.

That was why we chose them to be the winners, I told her. She turned to her two bridesmaids pleadingly. "You two will be sure to help me on the day, right? I know I'm going to be nervous."

"Well, every bride is nervous on the day, Kathy. That's just normal." Her chief bridesmaid Sam was her sister-in-law, too. "I was shaking when I married Larry. Half of the petals fell off the roses I was carrying when I walked down the aisle. Then I was scared someone would slip on them and get hurt – like on a banana skin!"

It was the first light moment in a series of meetings and we all joined in, over-enthusiastically trying to put the bride at ease.

"Well, we got a glimmer of a smile today," Marlon remarked after they had all left. "If we could get a couple more grins this affair just might not turn out like a funeral after all." He put the gowns onto the alterations rail and sighed. "I hope it turns out well for the couple but I have to say – I feel depressed every time that wee lassie walks in here. I'd need to do a somersault to cheer her up, maybe…"

For the first time I really thought about the whole prize and how it was affecting the couple. Most engaged couples would be jumping for joy but the reaction we were getting was subdued at best. Were we really doing them a favour…?

I hadn't added to Kathy's anxiety by mentioning to her that there would be a bit of a circus on the day of the wedding with press photographers and crowds of onlookers who had been following the newspaper competition. Certainly she would find out soon enough. The thought that all this would likely create more misgiving for her started to make me feel guilty, but I dismissed the negative vibes immediately. After all, wasn't that what weddings were all about – publicity, razzle dazzle and a big show for the cameras? Some people got a big kick out of all that. Besides, if a couple didn't want the spotlight of a big wedding, why enter a competition to win one?

The spotlight moment arrived soon enough a few weeks later and as the church bells chimed, our team, let alone all the other teams supporting the free wedding, were up and ready to deliver.

Suitably attired in my own new outfit, a duck-egg blue two piece silk crepe suit with matching fancy feather-trimmed chapeau fashioned by that highly acclaimed Glasgow Gallowgate designer Haughty Couture, I made my way past the crowds towards the church entrance. I was on my own temporarily, for Other Half had decided to personally chauffeur the bride and her dad to her local church in the Rolls Royce, and would join me inside afterwards and also later at the reception.   I posed confidently - I don't know why since I have always thought that any picture ever taken of me always bore a close semblance to Quasimodo or perhaps Cruella De Ville - and chatted to the groom and best man outside on the church steps. The weather was decent for early

October, dry…. and dry. Dry is all we need for most weddings – heat and sun can be a huge bonus for which we are occasionally grateful – but dry is usually good enough for wedding coordinators.

It was great to see throngs of people gather outside the church walls to witness our marketing miracle production – the free wedding competition outcome. Lana from the newspaper was there too, also appropriately attired in finery and big hat and agreeing that it had all been a great success from her standpoint. Her newspaper had increased its circulation, their advertising figures were thirty per cent higher than normal, so Lana had truly justified the cost of her elegant hat. When I conceded that our all-inclusive wedding package had taken off big time because of all the brouhaha, Lana became even more enthusiastic. Well, maybe we should do this every year, was the gist of her remarks. I was noncommittal. Let's see how all this goes first, I thought.

As guests of honour, Lana and I were seated way down the church, just a few rows back from the altar and where the groom and best man were now positioned. Of course the lads were demonstrating to one and all that the groom was early, keen and eager to take his humble position in the normal lengthy wait for the bride. His wait is usually lengthy because he has to be at church at least a half hour before the proceedings begin. This is unwritten law. And besides, the limos that drop off the guys normally have to head off again to the bride's house for pickups there. We could hear some activity at the entry and turned to see the bridesmaids scurrying about fussing with their accessories as they waited to welcome the bride. Traditionally she should follow her maids within five or ten minutes but it was almost the bewitching hour and our Cinderella had not appeared yet.

"Oh well, it's a bride's prerogative to be a teensy bit late," I said to Lana, hypocritically. I was being nice, for I absolutely think that the bride who deliberately arrives late does herself no favours. Sometimes it takes the rest of the afternoon and even into the evening reception to catch up, so tight is time at a wedding. Something always has to give.

Three o'clock came and went. At ten past the hour there was not so much as the brush of a bridal veil against the marble pillars at the front entry. What was going on? Nervously I focused on the fact that this was our show, our production - and the reviews were going to be terrible afterwards. I could foresee the headlines.

'Bridal Company can't get 'em to the church on time' and so on. 'Big package, really? Can the Bridal Company handle the pressure?'

These were my thoughts, so how self-absorbed was that? Shouldn't I have been wringing my hands instead about poor Kathy, agonizing how she was doing with those nerves or squirming that she could have ripped her veil, perhaps tripped down her front steps. Or even examine the possibility - horror of horrors – that she could have changed her mind?

"Please," I prayed, my eyes gazing upwards towards this ornate ecclesiastical ceiling. Yes, I took full advantage of the location itself, to pray for Kathy to show up. Well, not so much to pray, but rather to make the business deal of my career with the Man Upstairs….

"I promise I'll be soo-oo-oo good. I'll even start going to church to visit personally, not just in the usual professional capacity. Please. Just let Kathy show up and cut me a break."

The bride's mother was within reach two rows down, so since I was finding it almost impossible to stay still, I stepped out of my row and walked down to tap her on the shoulder, asking if the bride had been fine earlier. I began to wish I hadn't bothered.

"She was a wreck, honestly. I feel sick just thinking about it now. She wanted nothing to eat at all this morning, I was quite worried about her. I wonder what's happened?" This was the very discomforting response. I was not convincing in my rather cool reassurances to her either, but at least I tried.

The poor groom was being blatantly morally supported by his best man but it didn't prevent the pallor surfacing on his normally ruddy cheeks, or hamper him from having a late lunch snack on his fingernails. I imagined I heard him say to Clark, the best man: "I'll give her five minutes more to show up and if she doesn't, I'm outta here!" Now THAT would have been one heck of a newspaper headline. I started to chew my own recently manicured fingernails. Lana assured me the groom had uttered no such thing. I agreed and tried to bolster myself again.

"Of course he would never say a thing like that, I'm probably just delirious…."

By three twenty-five the feathers on my new hat were beginning to wilt from an excess of nervous perspiration and steam rising from my furrowed brow. Then suddenly there was hope. The chattering from the pews subsided a little as we detected a rustle of activity which appeared to be coming from the church entry.

The huge communal sigh of relief in that place of worship was so audible, it could have been heard at a wedding in the next village. But what I was mainly aware of was another more reassuring sound, the comforting click of the bride's high heels as she insinuated herself into her correct place at the top of the aisle, hanging onto and utilizing her dad as a physical and emotional buffer. And as she made her way down that extraordinarily long motorway of an aisle, she even managed a wry smile at her mother, suddenly looking as if she had won the lottery, as well as the wedding. Even poor Ken, the almost suicidal groom, seemed to find the will to live again. Just what we all wanted, a happy ending.

Lana sighed with relief, I sighed in order to blow one of my hat feathers back up where it belonged and Other Half sighed with exhaustion. He had just slipped into his seat beside me rolling his eyes intriguingly, making me look forward to finding out what had happened. But for now we had a wedding to witness.

As the ceremony ended and the now jubilant couple practically bounced back up the aisle wearing their shiny, new, free rings – I was enlightened. Other Half had handled the situation very well and I was proud of him.

"Honestly, I thought she was going to have a stroke," he told me, referring of course, to the bride. "I have never seen anything like it and her father was not much better - so she couldn't rely on him for support. You know how big that limo is? Well I felt it shuddering straightaway when she got into it at her home. I thought maybe the tyres needed rebalancing or something. But it was Kathy shaking in the back and when we got within a few hundred yards of the church she almost had a convulsion when she saw all the crowds there."

So what did he do? He offered to take them for a little drive, to let them cool down. There was no resistance from the back seat so he took off – to our house, our own residence less than three miles from the church.

"Well, it was only a short drive away and I had an idea. When we got there I excused myself for two minutes and came out of the house with a bottle of brandy and two glasses." Oh, right. My elegant and expensive Edinburgh Crystal ones…. "I practically commanded them to drink and settle themselves down while we took off real easy…."

He had obviously driven very slowly, indeed. I wondered why he hadn't got a ticket for loitering. But it worked, because as he drove and checked the mirror occasionally to view the once-traumatized passengers, things seemed to be improving gradually as the brandy was coaxed from its pretty bottle. He explained that it took quite a quantity of the golden nectar to achieve results.

It was incredible that I just couldn't see it before. I had not understood fully the extraordinary level of the bride's nerves and the true root cause of those nerves. The thing was that nobody in that whole family was truly prepared emotionally or financially for a big wedding just a few months hence. I reflected on how the majority of our weddings were booked at least a year ahead, which obviously gave families time to adjust on many levels. The high publicity profile we had inflicted, plus the extra personal pressure of having to financially limit the celebrations had taken its toll.

Yes, we could give out glittering, glamorous, free weddings all year long to deserving folk. But it was very difficult, without a generous time slot of personal pre-planning, to give them the mental fortitude to face the limelight, the crowds, the publicity shots that came with a free prize, let alone the fuss and dazzle of any regular wedding.

They had just not been ready for such a big do, particularly when it was a marketing promotion in disguise. We had created a wedding circus and expected them to perform in it like pros, when they had been merely amateurs with no time for rehearsal.

The wedding schedule had to be tightened up a little, but at least the pair were married now in spite of extreme nerves. Other Half had done the right thing, even if he had used up our personal supply of five star cognac.

"She did calm down big time," he went on, "but just to a normal level of nervousness, you understand." He looked at me, smiling. "After all, I can't do miracles."

Really? Personally, I thought he had.

Have Yourself a Merry Little Easter

Easter in the UK has got to be the most unique and bizarre of festivals because you just don't know what you are going to get, weather wise that is. The Easter I recall here was the extreme example – for the Easter bunny had wisely decided to stay in his rabbit hole for a little longer owing to the vast amount of snow in the west of Scotland. Children became inventive and had fun making snow bunnies instead of snowmen, using their mini Easter eggs for the buttons.

Unfortunately we had a diary full of weddings on that weekend - all made much more difficult because of the conditions. Somehow we managed and that is why I have no in-depth memory of their circumstance or outcome, for normality is quite forgettable, such is life. I do, however, have a strong recollection of the finale to that weekend, the abnormal Easter Monday Wedding.

Ironically we had very little responsibility to the Easter Monday Wedding, for our only duty was to provide limousines and chauffeur the wedding party to the church and afterwards, to the reception. The Easter Monday Wedding did not rely on us for gowns, kilts, cakes, photos, videos and so on – just for chauffeur services with three cars – two of our own silver Mercedes and one white Rolls Royce. This white car was sub contracted to us by another company. And we really should not have been compelled to subcontract this Rolls from the other company for the Easter Monday Wedding since we had a perfectly good, matching silver Rolls of our own to make up the set of limos. The bride, however, exercised her full prerogative of choice by declining this coordinated silver Rolls and declared that her ambition since childhood was to have a WHITE Rolls Royce to transport her on her big day. The silver Mercedes were perfectly tolerable. In fact the silver Mercedes were actually very nice, very nice indeed, but the Rolls just HAD to be white. She would just DIE if the bridal car was not a WHITE Rolls. She knew she was being silly and fussy, but she could not help herself. It would just HAVE to be white, for no other colour would do for the Easter Monday Wedding.

And so it came to pass on that Easter Monday that both Mercedes were cleaned and polished to a high standard before setting out on the snowy roads, roads which would certainly succeed in besmearing and soiling their turtle-waxed little bodies. At our end everything was good to go two hours before leaving our base. The interior of each car was immaculate with crisp white sheets lining the upholstery in order to protect the bridesmaids' gowns from the unfortunate dirt and slush outside. This was our normal practice with all vehicles. The main limo would also be presented perfectly for the bride, the Andrews Brothers would see to that with their white Rolls - of that I was quite sure. Also, all of the cars would have a cleaning kit in the boot that would enable the drivers to wipe down any hostile road mud or dirt collected en route to the wedding. These kits were very handy on days when there was snow and slush all around, days when it seemed to be one big dirt fight. For no matter how much elbow grease was put into the limos prior to a wedding, during damp conditions it was inevitable that they would arrive for their wedding pickups looking slightly soiled.

The drivers I employed were always instructed to help a bride wherever possible, to help lift her train when she exited or entered a car, guide her round a puddle like Sir Walter Raleigh or even try to arrest a veil about to blow off in the wind like a silky, fluffy kite. I saw it as being professionally helpful for I knew that a bride could not always rely on her bridesmaids to step up to the plate. I always felt that bridesmaids – and particularly chief bridesmaids – could do much more to help the star of the show on her big day. After four decades in the wedding business, we regularly saw little support for the bride from female attendants who were too busy preening themselves to help out. Often we could see this coming way before the big day at dress selections and fittings in the shop when some bridesmaids made it clear their appearance and outfit came first. Not all bridesmaids are condemned here, just a few….

I remember one mature, glamourous bride who came to me to do her whole wedding. Olivia was a feisty Italian lady, with four grown-up beautiful (like herself) daughters who took forever fussing in the salon over their choice of bridesmaid dresses. Olivia lost it with them – totally. I can still hear her yelling loudly at them in her best Neapolitan gutsy accent: "Look, the dresses are forra MY wedding. Thees ees notta YOUR day! Eet eesa MY day, MY day, see!" They got the message but I digress, for this is not a textbook on 'what to do and what not to do for your wedding'. I'll save that for another time.

Andrews Brothers was a limo company we had done business with for many years. We provided cars for them if they were overly busy and vice versa, which meant helping each other out during the hectic wedding season and trusting each other to give a good service and protect our respective reputations. The brothers were a family of four and worked with beloved patriarch Mr Andrews senior who ruled the roost, by all accounts. Their main business was a cash and carry on the outskirts of our town and their large expanse of property with huge car park enabled them to also house their secondary business – wedding car hire. Their fleet incorporated silver cars, burgundy cars and white, whilst our fleet was all silver and very coordinated indeed.

We also shared drivers, and more than one of Andrews' full time employees in the cash and carry acted as weekend chauffeurs for the weddings for both of our companies. The Andrews lads were all huge, all telegraph pole tall but with hearty girths. They were great fun personalities and this rubbed off on their drivers, for we had many a laugh at weddings, when I would cross their paths as I performed other wedding tasks. And there was nothing I enjoyed more than when I personally chauffeured at a wedding where they would be swapping stories and gossiping, something I found most men enjoyed heartily. The Andrews did not seem to hoard their height for themselves alone, since every driver they employed looked like another family member with the same distinctive stature. Being a smurf myself I always felt like a nippy little Lilliputan amongst a group of gentle Gullivers when we worked together. Not one of the brothers or their drivers were shorter than six feet four inches at least. I know this reeks of Neanderthal maths but I am not a metric maid.

With just a miserly two hours to spare before leaving for the Easter Monday Wedding I had a phone call from Donny, the chief Andrews brother. It was not good news.

"You'll never guess what's happened! The old boy has just five minutes ago reversed one of the vans out of the depot into the Rolls Royce and damaged it. It was sitting in the car park, all clean, polished and ready to go! We've warned my father umpteen times not to reverse any of the fleet – he's hopeless at that stuff now, but he just won't listen! God, we won't be able to do the wedding with you now, I'm really sorry…"

I told him I would be right over and hung up. Words and explanations were not enough so I had to see this for myself. Heading out of town to the Andrew's depot I felt very pessimistic and a little desperate. How bad would the damage be and why was I bothering to go over and see this at all, for plainly we could not send a damaged car out to a wedding. Ten minutes later I swept into their premises looking for a solution to an impossible situation. Sure enough there was the gorgeous white Rolls, a Cinderella carriage, sitting there in the cold icy sunshine and almost camouflaged against the deep white snow not yet cleared from the depot car park. Two of Andrews' chauffeurs, Pat and Big Matt were rigged out in their smart grey uniforms and were standing next to the vehicle. It was flashing into my head that the Andrews must have yet another wedding elsewhere, since there were two drivers. They acknowledged me by nodding dourly as I strode towards them.

"The car looks great and you guys appear ready to go, so where is the damage?" I asked as I walked around the limo twice, slowly and carefully. There seemed to be no problem at all. I put my hands on my hips and demanded an answer from somebody. Was this a joke? We all enjoyed a laugh but come on! Time was getting tighter for today's wedding. The lads were looking almost smug and I was running out of patience. "Are you kidding me, where's the problem?"

As I uttered these last few words, the two chauffeurs stepped aside and suddenly all was revealed. There it was. I was shocked to see one beauty of a bash right in the middle of the front passenger's door. I may not have caught it before with the two giants blocking it, but now that it was showcased, it seemed to assume all the proportions of the Grand Canyon.

"You see, you never even noticed it," bossman Donny said as he strode towards me. He had obviously just come out of the office.

I hadn't noticed him at first but unfortunately I HAD noticed the dreadful dent. It was unquestionably obvious and I told Donny as much.

"Yeah, I know. But not when the men are standing in front of it." It was true. Both of those guys could have hidden a Boeing 747 if required. Donny looked almost pleased with himself. "So what I can do is this – I'll send both drivers – at no extra expense to you, of course and they will be on their guard at all times to defend the dent. Nobody who cares will see it, trust me. Guaranteed!" He put his hands on his knees and squatted down a wee bit towards me grinning, as if I were a small child and he was rewarding me with a lollipop. "So there you are. What do you say?"

There was no time to mess around – I had to make a decision. Would I take one of the drivers back to our base to drive our lovely UN-dented silver Rolls which the Easter Monday Wedding bride detested or would I take a chance on the white, slightly imperfect version? Intuitively I leaned towards the white limo. It was the bride's choice and she was much less likely to have a nervous breakdown with the white car than with the silver. Plus these two big burly drivers just might succeed in hiding the dent. After all, even I hadn't noticed the damage on keen and forewarned inspection. This was my gut feeling. As we had less than two hours before the ceremony itself there was no time to involve another limo company. Most of my contacts for white limos were in Glasgow anyway - so preparation time, terrible road conditions and distance would have severely limited their ability to help out.

"Ok, let's go," I said to Donny and five minutes later I set off back to base with the white limo trailing me. We would depart as a team from our base - and a true team we would have to be today.

Archie, our other Mercedes driver was filled in on the situation before we all left together on the eight mile journey to Hamilton and the Easter Monday Wedding. I could sense his disapproval of the Great Dent Deception.

"Well," he said ruefully. "If anybody asks me about that big beauty of a bash at least I can say it wisnae me who did it!"

Archie was our senior driver. He had been with the company for longer than any of the others and he was more advanced in years. The term 'senior' had an equivocal meaning for him, so he would refer to himself as the 'chief' driver. This enabled him to lord it over the others like a big shot even though he was the shortest of them all, barely five feet in height. But Archie was not really a small man – he was a big man in every other aspect but height. He was a very reliable honest worker and since he was old enough to be my uncle, we adopted him as such and the family enjoyed his company at our table for dinner regularly. He was a veteran of WW11 and would regale us with fascinating stories of his exploits in Italy and North Africa where he drove large trucks. As a history lecturer, Other Half found the war stories to be fascinating, which they were, but I laughed when he would start one of his military stories with the famous sit-com line: 'During the war....'

There was one occasion when he was driving the main bridal car for us. Unfortunately the bride's strapless dress conceded to gravity and dropped down leaving her boobs on display as she was just exiting the car for the church. Archie thought quickly and grabbed the white sheet covering the limo's rear seat, holding it over her and shielding her modesty. The bridesmaids ran quickly from the church steps to help and apparently everything was sorted out satisfactorily, although Archie was blushing more than the poor bride. After this, all the other drivers would tease him. "Hey, Archie. Next week I'm going to ask if I can drive wi' you at your wedding. You get all the good jobs!"

This Easter Monday all three cars were parked neatly outside the big modern church and so far it had gone well. Not one person, guest or photographer had cottoned onto our dent. Probably the freezing cold weather plus the nervous frenzy of the wedding itself meant there was no hanging about – just a few photos of the bride and dad inside the Rolls which had been parked strategically so the dent was on the other side. And whilst Ben opened doors and such, Bill would act as defending decoy. It was a bad movie, but the actors were good.

Conveniently, the fact that there were TWO chauffeurs in the vehicle seemed to impress the family. Everyone considered the extra fully smart uniformed chauffeur a plus factor and I have to say it did look impressive and not suspicious in any way.

We chauffeurs did not relish hanging about that cold day but once we dropped off the party at the church we had no choice. This was a full mass wedding and a painfully long time to wait inside the cars to avoid the freezing conditions outside. The wait was particularly uncomfortable for Archie and me. You see, in those olden days I was a wanton, wicked woman who smoked. My weekly consumption of ciggies would be about three packs a week so it wasn't too bad. I constantly threatened to quit but my 'absolutely-necessary- for- my- sanity' regular trips to warmer climes in the Med kept me puffing away. From these trips I had stashes of duty-free fags to use up but just as I was about to drain that lot and give up for good, guess what? I would be off travelling again and return with more of the nicotine sticks. Big vicious circle.

That ice-cold day, I used the old excuse 'a cigarette would heat me up' but in order to be warmed up I would have to step out of the wedding car, for as much as I wanted a cigarette I would never smoke inside any of the cars. Verboten, absolutely. Archie was verging on chain smoker. It's a wonder he did not have a wee chimney coming out the top of his head but this aside, Archie knew the rules and adhered rigidly to them. If I had ever sniffed smoke from any of those vehicles there would have been big trouble. That Arctic day at the Easter Monday Wedding, we tried to smoke outside, honestly. It looked very pretty outdoors because of the sunny, cloudless sky – but it was a deathly, icy cold. A day when you could get a sunburn and frostbite at the same time. The smoking attempt failed miserably – but we didn't give up, no sir.

"I just can't enjoy this Archie, I'm going back in the car." I was shivering - so what was the point.

Archie had a brainwave, bearing in mind the cold had probably caused his brain and any other vital organs to shrink dramatically. "You see that kind of hallway inside the church, I'm going to check it out. Maybe we would be alright to smoke there."

I wasn't so sure about illicit lighting up inside a church but I did not discourage him on his exploration, either. When he returned from his scouting I took over. He had said there was a corridor to the left of the hallway – a long corridor that contained several doors.

"Let's go and check it out, no harm in that, eh?" I chipped in weakly.

Pat and Matt voiced their disapproval but I rejected this with mock laughter, giving them a glare of 'who are you to talk, disguising the dent' and so on. Archie and I stealthily made our way down the long corridor, having decided to start at the very end, to examine the last room first, the room furthest away from any ecclesiastical, nuptial proceedings currently inside the church itself and hopefully the least likely place to be detected. We were in luck. The last tiny room was a cleaner's room, a utility room that would be absolutely superfluous just now, in the middle of a wedding. There was nothing much inside, the only occupants being an assortment of mops and buckets, but we still had barely room enough to squeeze in there, close the door and light up. It was a glorified cupboard.

We were halfway through a very welcome drag of nicotine, all the time whispering softly to avoid detection, when suddenly… whoosh! The door flew open and a tall, young, very red-headed priest stood there in his robes, glowering and literally crimson faced with rage. Obviously his red hair did not belie his disposition and he looked as if he would literally explode. The whole scenario was reminiscent of school and being caught smoking behind the bike shed by the headmaster. Just worse….

We gasped and extinguished the rogue cigarettes in seconds. This appeared to be of no consequence to the enraged priest. Before we could say 'Players, please' he grabbed both of us by the scruff of our freshly starched white business collars with both hands and literally dragged us back down the corridor towards the front entry of the church, all the while venting his anger by uttering incoherent maledictions – I swear it must have been priest profanity, exclusively used by them.

Archie and I were already struggling to retain both our balance and our last scrap of dignity when the final affront came. The priest released our neckhold and adopted another violent tactic by shoving us both unceremoniously out of the door and down the church steps. Fortunately they had been cleared of snow.

I was ashamed and furious at the same time. Of course I knew we were very wrong to have done this idiotic thing but as a priest he should have understood the existence of imbeciles in this world, simpletons who should be forgiven for their tobacco- troubled sins. He could have taken pity, inquired about our chromosome levels and then given us a jolly good telling off, huh! Violence was uncalled for.

Pat and Matt were just getting out of the Rolls at this time, in anticipation of the wedding party's exit. Pat was in decoy position, weakened by the fact that he could not stand still for laughing at our plight.

Archie and I were troopers. We tried bravely to put the incident behind us, picked up our last remnants of pride and got on with the less exciting balance of the troublesome Easter Monday wedding.

Later that evening after a hot bath and a glass of Merlot both of which helped to recover my inalienable right of dignity – I received a phone call.

"It's someone from the Catholic Church," my teenage son threw out carelessly. I had not enlightened him about his mother's shameful 'behind the bike shed' exploit earlier that day. Some things were best left alone.

But I was still perplexed. Why would the Pope be calling me at this time? With the time difference, wasn't it past his bedtime? So he had found out about my delinquency already and I would be ex-communicated.

Then realization kicked in. Hold on, I was not a member of the RC church to begin with, so how could I be? My trembling hand took the phone and like an adult, I declared my identity. I hoped the Pope would speak to me in English, not Latin. I didn't even have an O-Level in Latin. Pity they didn't have a French Pope anymore. I had had six years of Higher French which would have helped in this situation.....

"Hello, this is Father McCrone from St Aiden's Church in Hamilton."

"Oh!" I was just slightly gobsmacked. "Yes?" The shock had me fumbling for something intelligible to say.

"I have to apologise for my handling of the situation today," he continued quietly. Long pause. "I'm afraid I lost my temper completely."

Handling was the right word. He had certainly man-handled both Archie and me which was technically, politically incorrect even in the early 90's. Yes, he had applied physical abuse which was deplorable but I knew the criterion and put my hands up. This was metaphorically, of course - for I was still nervously clutching the telephone with two trembling hands.

It was an indisputable fact that Archie and I had taken a wicked chance in God's house and we both had a feeling that the house mortgagee would not have approved. No matter what, we were wrong. Even the priest's conciliatory stance could not nurse my guilt.

I may have felt all this but I did warn the priest in pretty snippy fashion to mind his temper in future. I mean, I had to take SOME advantage of this moment, for how often does a person get to preach to a cleric? Although I have to admit that over the four decades, I have had my moments of being frank with many clergymen.   He agreed wholeheartedly that he had sinned. This was just as well for I could not, considering the location of our sin, even think of using the well-worn line: 'I've been thrown out of better places than this!'

Of course the cigarette story made the wedding car circuit for ages afterwards and we were both teased mercilessly by chauffeurs from far and wide. My normal businesslike stance had taken a severe denting, just like the car door. "Any smokes, love?" or "You know, I'll have to give up the ciggies – not doctor's orders, priest's orders…"

Bridal ER

'Wedding Accident and Emergency'. That should have been added to our huge midnight blue and gold, glossy shop sign declaring that we were a one stop bridal shop. It sometimes seemed that for our local community and beyond we were first responders for wedding emergencies – some minor and others pretty significant.

There were so many occasions when we had to step in quickly to rescue a wedding from disaster. Invariably weddings that we had NOT been involved in ran to us - as the local wedding establishment - to sort out crazy problems. On many occasions we were brought in to quickly set a bride up with a fresh veil after someone, usually the bride's mum, on the morning of the wedding had decided to iron the bridal veil – a total no-no-no-no never-do-it-act of lunacy. The first remedy to apply in this case would be to hang a creased veil in the bathroom with a clip hanger to absorb the steam from someone's shower or bath. Or a spray mist of clean cold water dried off with a cool hairdryer, works too.

Of course wedding dresses were next on the triage. A nerve-racking last minute repair to a wedding gown that had also suffered at the hands of the evil electric iron was not uncommon either. Fortunately we had a magical work basket overflowing with spare parts – sequined butterflies or lace flowers and so on which could be utilized only if appropriate. A busy wedding dress with sequins and pearls and lace is much easier to rescue than a perfectly plain one, as you can imagine.

'The dog ate my wedding slippers!' This A & E did happen occcasionally but thankfully we had a healthy stock of satin wedding shoes in all sizes to help substitute. Wedding shoe disasters were very avoidable, but unfortunately they still happened. Why? Although brides tended to hang well covered gowns high over the bedroom or wardrobe door, away from chocolate fingered toddlers, their shoes would often be left sitting on the carpet in the bedroom. We learned that young dogs love new shoes and often mistook them for chew toys….

If we could, we would help. Most of these emergencies were not from our own clients, and I knew why. No customer ever left our premises with delicate veils and dresses without being advised how to store, hang or care for them properly. Besides the care advice, there was absolutely no necessity for using an iron on the dresses and accessories we provided, for they had already been thoroughly professionally steamed by one of our staff in the salon. The very patient Adrienne was our part time employee whose job it was to take care of steaming and pressing all clothing leaving the shop either for purchase or hire. These items were then bagged securely on a hanger ready to hang in the car or at least spread out on the back seat. I was convinced that some brides' mothers just couldn't balance their conscience in NOT ironing the wedding dress. You know, the type of soul who irons the tea towels....

Male clients were by no means exempt from disasters and in fact our staff had to watch them very carefully since they were notorious for having casual attitudes towards their hired wedding gear. No wonder our menswear manager Marlon regularly complained of his nerves. Well forewarned to either try on in the salon or alternatively check outfits immediately on arriving home with them, this cut no dice with many guys. We had visions of them heading back home, hanging the kilt or suit outfit over the back of a chair and then heading off to the pub, or the golf course. Have you guessed? Yes, the outfit wouldn't be given a second thought until the big day and an hour or so before the wedding when a half-soaked usher or groom would suddenly realise he had banged on some beef over the celebratory buildup to the wedding and that buttons would not button or buckles refused to buckle. It would be a panic for us to find alternative sizes or move buttons and buckles with minutes, not even hours, to spare before the ceremony. Goodness knows how we managed to overcome many of these self-induced disasters, but we did. I have no memory of anyone being left entirely in the lurch. I recall that as a safeguard Marlon even had a little flyer printed off for clients to magnet to the family fridge with a 'how to' instruction and a 'must do' warning.

The juniors in the wedding party caused many a stir, too. We had stress-filled experiences of flower girls tearing their dresses - mostly by accident, occasionally by design. One little trainbearer decided to 'colour in' her aunt's ivory satin frock with wax crayon just hours before the ceremony. Unforgettable was the three year-old pageboy who tried to flush his wee kilt down the toilet on the morning of the big day. Perhaps it was part of his toilet training and fortunately no plumber was called – just us. We had to come up with another last minute kilt to replace the sodden one. It would be tedious to go on with the list. Instead here is an example of wedding A & E which affected a very sweet client of ours and involved a mad dash over the Scottish border…..

I took a long last sip from my coffee cup as I heard the group coming into the salon. It was the first appointment of the day and not yet nine am – a problem for me personally since my body rhythms didn't generally click in till about ten o'clock midweek. I was intrigued by the special request for my presence which usually meant a problem of some sort. Maureen, Adrienne, Jinty or Marlon were all more than capable of handling dress fittings so there had to be an exceptional issue afoot and THAT did make me a little nervous. As the owner, the buck stopped with me and I never shied away from it. If there was a problem with business then I had to confront it head on, no matter how unpleasant the situation was. But I had no idea what the issue was in this case – it was a total mystery.

Three bridesmaids and a little flower girl were to be fitted for a wedding almost five weeks hence and there appeared to be some urgency on the part of the bride to get it done. She had insisted on bringing it forward a few days and we wondered why.   Three to four weeks before was usually final fitting time and our staff was more than capable of handling any circumstance. But there seemed to be an unhealthy haste, an uncalled for urgency from the bride who had been suspiciously discreet on the telephone. Could one of the bridesmaids be pregnant and showing some extra weight? Had the chief bridesmaid gained a couple of stone from that new extra cheese and pepperoni pizza diet? Perhaps the bride had had a change of heart regarding the colour or style of the bridesmaid dresses? We had come across it all before, so what this time?

As the bridesmaids went off for their fittings with Jinty and Adrienne I concentrated exclusively on our troubled looking main girl. Roslyn the bride smiled at me with what looked like relief when I took a seat beside her on our big luxurious sofa in the centre of the salon. The smile was misleading - as I drew closer I could see the anxiety in her blue eyes.

"You have to help me with this one, it's a disaster."

She was definitely struggling to hold back the tears.

It was no disaster that I knew of. We were producing almost all of the wedding except for limousines and the wedding dress, so all the plans were watertight. Roslyn's marriage location and reception was a small castle hotel several miles away and the main party was spending the night before at the venue, hence no need for cars at all. However, the bridesmaid dresses being fitted today, well timed before the big date, turned out to be an opportunity for the bride to reveal her newly-found crisis, that of her wedding gown. I knew that the dress was out of our hands, and then recalled that it was being created by a relative who prided herself on her tailoring and dressmaking skills. And this, I soon discovered, was the 'disaster'.

"I don't know what to do. Look!"

At the end of the long sofa she had placed a homemade, but very adequate, large white cotton dress cover. She reached for it, stood up and with a visibly shaking hand discarded the cover. Firmly attached to a padded white lace hanger was her wedding dress, now being offered for my inspection. I tried to take in every detail of the garment, the supposed dream dress that Roslyn now found so offensive and at first it was difficult to connect with the problem. Initially the gown seemed well cut and the fabric appeared to be a fine, off-white shantung silk. Then I examined the fabric more closely. Oh, no... I silently scolded my defective morning body rhythms for being slow, very slow, because I realized the material was definitely not shantung, rather a low quality polyester fake. Even worse, the detachable train had been lined with tacky, ultra-white nylon fabric. It was certainly not Vera Wang. It was not even Wera Vang. It was very bad.

I employed my best poker face but it didn't help. Roslyn couldn't hold back the cornflower blue floodgates one minute longer. Dealing with this one, which she had discovered only the night before at her aunt's home, was just too much for her. As I looked again at the dress my mind was racing with options on how to salvage the situation but I knew instinctively that as bad as it first looked, probably not all had been revealed yet. How many more complications were lurking there – in the seedy seams of this little dress that could potentially cause a nervous breakdown for this unfortunate bride, let alone myself. I dismissed the thought and determined to be positive.

It was challenging to act assured since Roslyn seemed to be in the depths of despair. "It's absolutely awful. Look, look at the beadwork – a total mess!" She glared at the poor little dress as if it were public enemy number one.

She was right about the embellishment. It's not impossible, but extremely difficult, for the average seamstress to emulate top designs, particularly when it comes to adding sequins and pearls and so on. Regrettably, this kind of scenario wasn't overly shocking to staff at the salon for we had encountered similar experiences before. On booking any wedding, if we heard that the gran was making the dress, or perhaps that uncle Roger was doing the photos, or a friend whose specialty was ordinarily baking delicious chocolate brownies was challenging herself to create a four tier wedding cake, we cringed a little. No, we cringed a lot. It's lovely to have helpful friends and family, but not when they unwittingly cause catastrophes.

As far as this dress was concerned, the application of beadwork let it down badly. Ashamedly, the gorgeous pearl-laden creations we see in bridal shop windows and all admire are normally the result of blindness-inducing hours of labour in sweatshops all over the far east. This applies not only to mid-range gowns but also at the top end of the market, too. There is not much tolerance level for such precise hand work in our own western society, particularly when it comes to amateur seamstress aunts.

The dreaded question finally came.

"Can you fix it?"

Roslyn paused for a few seconds, staring at me as I implored my brain to send me placating words of wisdom. She let me off the hook a little by answering the question herself.

"Somehow I don't think so – and you know, it doesn't even fit so well, either…"

I urged her to slip into the gown in the men's area – it was quiet and isolated from her party who were noisily rejoicing in the success of their own fittings. It was all such a drastic contrast to our bride's despair that it became eerily disheartening. I took the dress while she placed a couple of pretty, feminine-looking lilac paper carrier bags down into the furthest away cubicle.

"My lingerie and my shoes," she explained a little unnecessarily.

I was glad she had remembered. It was encouraging to see she had asserted herself enough to think of this, even in her upset state, for many girls managed to overlook these vital components of a successful fitting. On occasions we had been forced to cancel arrangements if the proper undergarments weren't with the client. Fittings without the correct tool kit of bra, shoes and hold-me-in knickers were generally a waste of time.

"Well, it zips up and it seems to be a decent general fit, although I can see some room for improvement. But come out to the main salon for a proper look in the natural light." Electric light can be forgiving whilst broad daylight – sometimes unfortunately – tells the truth.

I genuinely was attempting to be unshockable, even reassuring. I held the separate train of the dress as we made our way through the cubicle area to the main salon. Nothing would be overlooked there, on the dais near our big full length cheval mirror and the front panoramic bay window with natural daylight streaming through. Sure enough, as I looked closely I discovered a front dart that was not perfectly straight and appeared to be misaligned with the other. The gown had been cut in a princess line which tends to make even more obvious that type of error. Strangely enough, Roslyn seemed not to notice it, probably being involved in surveying the many other demerits of the dress. I mentally shelved the faux-pas for later. We had enough to be going on with.

"Look at the neckline," she sighed as she tugged at the draped material around the cowl style top. "It's just not sitting properly. One side keeps falling off my shoulder and the other side just sticks up like a sore thumb."

The eyes turned to overflowing swimming pools again. They were such nice eyes, too. Roslyn would definitely have fitted as a candidate for one of the portraits on our salon walls, I thought. Photographers tended to offer us some of their work to display and of course the most stunning of our brides would be chosen. I hoped that when this was all settled she would eventually end up there in pride of place. We would see. She was not tall, but petite and fair-haired, her short punky crop enhanced by some professional blonde highlights. She certainly had the face of an angel and that pore-free complexion was a perfect setting for the crystal blue eyes – eyes which right now were exhausting my box of tissues. I had to offer some advice - and quickly.

"Okaa-aay. I can see there are issues here. So let's look at all the details of the dress first. Number one is the choice of material. Not much we can do to change that, of course. Number two is the cut of the gown itself, another impossibility. Also you must bear in mind that there are only four weeks plus to your wedding."

She winced as I said the last part.

"So if you believe that these two problems don't matter then we will try to tackle some fresh beading for you and tidy up the fit."

I had been very frank but kept my attention on Roslyn's face the whole time. I hated to be responsible for heart attacks or faintings, but instead a look of optimism appeared, or was I deluding myself?

"Remember, if you decide the cut and fabric doesn't matter...." Slight pause. "What do you think?"

Roslyn looked at me in almost disbelief. She was very emotional. "You know, last night when I tried it on at my aunt's house I could see it was bad. But as I stand here in broad daylight I realise for the first time just how awful it is."

She almost willingly started to choke on her own tears. She pulled the last tissue from the box and blew her nose – not terribly winsomely. She was gobbling so much paper she was becoming eco-unfriendly. I popped off to the back shop to put some more coffee on, collect another box of tissues and give her a thinking space. By the time I returned she had seemed to settle down.

"You want to know how I feel about rescuing this dress? It's beyond hope, you know it is." She pointed to the front panel in disgust. "Can you believe this – the vertical panels don't even align!"

Ah, I thought. She finally noticed. I was relieved that she was forming her own snagging list and she was getting no arguments from my side.

"Well, we can look carefully at our stock of dresses here. But you would have to take from our existing dress rail samples – it is far too late to order now."

There was absolutely no chance of ordering at this stage since all of our suppliers demanded a sixteen to twenty-four weeks minimum notice for gowns, depending on the season. Our bride was confronted with the choice of what we had already in the shop so it was vital to point this out.

"I know we've nothing in stock that bears a strong likeness to your choice of design, so it would be start afresh time, okay? You need to have an open mind." This was a big ask. Almost all brides have a mental image of themselves in the dream dress they have chosen and are usually reluctant to shred it at the drop of a hat.

Although her face seemed to be looking down at her dreaded dress, the eyes were peering up appealingly towards me. "I think I already know the answer, but is there a chance your salon could MAKE my dress before the day?"

I had to put a damper on the possibility.

"No chance at all, Roslyn. We do produce bespoke gowns - but we need months of notice before the date. Our dressmakers are overladen with alterations as it is during the season. Believe me, for your purposes, you would be better to have a ready gown."

Roslyn nodded slowly. I suspected she seemed open to ideas and had slightly recovered emotionally by now. Was it possible that the huge hurdle of accepting the rejection of her original gown had steadied her nerves enough to accept another path to peace of mind? Sometimes we wedding producers felt like counsellors. Anyhow, without excessive cajoling, she had seen herself that the dress had many imperfections, probably just too many to overlook or remedy.

Off we went on the big search, just the two of us and I was wishing that the two assistants were here to help but they were still busy with the bridesmaids. I finally called on Marlon, our only male salon employee. He had been attending to highlandwear orders in the office and phone calls to arrange men's fittings, but I suggested he shelf that for a while.

I explained the situation and of course he was horrified.

"Will they never learn? When I hear about homemade wedding dresses it sets my nerves on edge."

Of course Marlon's edgy nerves were a constant source of entertainment for the rest of us in the salon. They were a diversion when we all felt the stress of high season wedding production and he would start to drop gossip all over the salon floor. We should have swept his bitchy tittle tattle right under the carpet – but instead we unashamedly lapped it up. I warned him to tread carefully around a bride whose own nerves were hanging by a thread.

"She's struggling with the reality that her dream dress is no longer a dream. So Marlon, be extra nice."

"Hmmm. I know, I know….but how bad is this little ex-dream, eh?"

He suddenly glimpsed the homespun dress hanging in the main salon, alone and rejected. I wondered for a moment if his eyes would pop out of their sockets, or had he been over zealous with the eyeliner again…..

"In the name of….." He mumbled, and walked over to the offending article, to feel if it was real. He looked amazed and it really hit me just how bad this little creation was.

"She could always keep it for a dress up party, or Halloween," he murmured, arms folded high in front as if to shield himself from the horror of it.

"Don't dare say that to her," I stage whispered. "Our job is to forget this," and I pointed to the polyester problem, "so that we can move on and satisfy our devastated customer with a beautiful new gown, ok? I need you to haul out dresses and I'll attend to her in the men's cubicles. It's nice and quiet there just now. Let's go."

"Ok. But for heaven's sake let's put the cover back on that wee frock before my vertigo kicks in again. If another customer comes in they'll think we're selling tat!"

He covered the nightmare then darted off to the rails, challenged to deliver THE dress to our emotionally fragile client. And he did well. Roslyn was open to every suggestion, compromising on necklines or fabric, experimenting with shades of ivory and white. But no. There were some great results but nothing that set her heart a flutter. It is often said that choosing a wedding dress is like choosing a husband – that a woman just KNOWS when the choice is right. I would add that the bride will hopefully have many years to work on a husband to shape him even more towards her idea of perfection. But with a dress, it is what it is. Short of a couple of minor alterations to length or width it is already complete, so it has to present itself as perfect immediately. A tough challenge, indeed.

Roslyn was not trying to be difficult, but she was struggling. Two of the bridesmaids had completed their fittings and stayed on to support her.

"I really want to get my dress here," she told the girls. "The idea of traipsing around Glasgow is a nightmare so soon to the wedding day. But if that's what it takes, I've no choice."

It seemed pretty hopeless. Then I thought of a possibility.

"Hold on a few minutes, I have an idea."

I set off for the back office to scan our files of recent dress catalogues from suppliers. A thorough check of last season's lines - and there it was. A dress similar to Roslyn's original choice, which we ourselves had never stocked, was beckoning to me from its glossy magazine pages. It was not exactly the same, but it was as near to heaven as I could reach at this stage.

Our bride was sceptically looking at herself in a glamourous white, sparkly fishtail lace number which was definitely NOT her. I handed over the catalogue.

Roslyn seemed excited by the photo and Marlon was just happy to take the fishtail sample back to the rails, judging by his frown.

She shared her first, genuine, happy grin with us when she saw the out of date catalogue. "Well, that's amazing. It's satin, not shantung silk but it has the same lines and neckline, too. Do you think I could get it, what about the deadline on ordering?"

"I don't know. This catalogue is almost a museum piece. It's full of extinct dresses, mostly. It's a longshot but every supplier has a leftover supply of samples they don't sell. I could always phone the company to check. And we need a size ten or twelve which most samples come in. We could even work with a fourteen at a pinch…."'

Marlon was back and listening in. He looked at her trim figure. "And we would have to pinch it in bigtime!"

I could still see that her eyes were red-rimmed. "Do you want me to find out?"

"Absolutely. Go for it. I'll have to phone my mum who is probably having kittens by now. She couldn't get away from her teaching job today to come with me – it was all so last minute."

Roslyn's sister Kate had her four-year old flowergirl daughter with her and was keen to exit, understandably.

"I'd love to stay and give advice but it would be better not to."

She nodded down to the little girl by her side.

"So I'm going off to lunch or the park or anywhere else but here," she laughed. "Then you can all have peace, right Jolie?"

Her daughter was ready to leave, for sure.

"Come on, wee lamb. Bye, bye, ladies. And Roslyn, best of British!"

I phoned this particular supplier in Newcastle. Amber Gowns was a well established, family owned firm and I knew the owners personally from the trade shows we attended in Harrogate, Yorkshire. The owners Alf and Greta Green were honest, down to earth people, easy to do business with and had proved to be trustworthy suppliers over the years. Their no nonsense approach meant you could trust their company to give an accurate window for deliveries. That no one was let down was a vital factor in this high pressure business.

I highlighted the problem to Alf.

"Ye what, hinny? Ye want us to search through the archives for an out of season frock, are ye mad?"

"Now, Alf." I hoped I could persuade him. "I know for a fact that you want us to take some of your old samples for promotional sales. Remember you spoke to me about it last month? You've got boxes of them with nowhere else to go and for the right price I might take lots of them from you for a special summer sale."

"Now this particular gown is a one-off, that's true. But Alf, come on! A dress like this will end up in one of those bargain boxes anyway. It won't take that long to find it, if you have it. Then we can talk about my buying some more, huh?"

"Aa've never heard the like. It's beyond my apprehension. All this and ah haven't even had a brew yet. Aa've been overcome with orders all morning."

I smiled at the phone. It was funny when he started to 'malaprop' which was usually when he got excited.

"Can I phone you back in a couple of hours and get the answer? Time isn't on our side."

"Alright. So long as you're ready to take some more old lines off our hands, ah'll get Greta and the girls to check this one out for you. But ah'm not promisin' anything…."

"Try to let me know as soon as, Alf. The poor girl's a wreck."

"We'll try not to keep her in suspenders too long. Ah'll phone you in a coupla hours."

Roslyn breathed a sigh of relief, for now. Off she went for lunch with instructions to return at two o'clock for the good or bad news.

The phone rang at five past two just as I was about to call Alf. It was Amber Gowns and the man himself.

"We have B60321. And wad ye believe it, it's a size twelve. But it isn't white, it's champagne. Nearly white, as ye know."

Great. I was sure Roslyn would go for it. I told Alf I would call him after speaking with the bride. A few minutes later she came back to the salon. I showed her a fabric sample of the colour that Amber qualified as 'champagne'.

"Yes, this shade would be nice," as she ran it between her fingers thoughtfully. "To tell the truth I really had gone off white, anyway. Maybe I've just gone off anything to do with that dress," as she nodded in the direction of our 'wee frock' still hanging there sadly. "It wouldn't affect the basic structure of our plans or colour theme, would it?" She looked uncertain but I reassured her.

"Not really. I can advise the baker to reflect it in the cake icing which hasn't been done yet, anyway. Your invitations were white, but they're already gone. But honestly, Roslyn – champagne is not a drastic colour change with the Amber dresses. The change will be of little consequence, if it happens…."

Smiles, smiles and more smiles flashed around the shop again. Back to the phone.

"Alf, that sounds great. Now when can you get it off to me?"

"In a couple o' days normally. But you know about the postal and delivery strike, don't you? It starts in the morn and could go on for days. Then we'll have slow backlogs. So most of our customers are picking up their orders. Where are you based again, pet?"

I reminded him of our location near Glasgow and he scoffed.

"Ye're only just around the corner, hinny. Ye' could be here in less than three hours and settle this dress plus take home the samples we agreed. Tomorrow?"

"I'll call you right back again," and hung up. This sartorial tennis game was very tiring indeed. And I had forgotten completely about the postal strike – which had been all over the news.

Roslyn was not just sympathetic to the idea of travelling down with me to Tyneside, she was champing at the bit.

What had sounded extreme at first was now beginning to make sense. I mumbled to myself but Roslyn was listening in big time. "Mmmm….It would mean you could try this dress on to make sure plus I could pick up some stock."

"Right," she agreed. "And I want to drive. I'll take my dad's big Volvo to let you save your strength for my problems. Hurrah, I think I'm saved!"

Next morning at eleven o'clock we were pulling into the car park outside Amber's premises, a relatively new warehouse near the Tyne.

Alf was there to greet us and ushered us through a huge stock room into a small, messy little office cramped with files, fabric samples and catalogues. He disappeared then came back with the prize offering and presented it theatrically.

"Here ye are. Frock B60321 in champagne. Aye, your lucky day, lucky day. We want everyone to be happy. Don't want no cardinal arrests here, bejeez! Now, what do ye take in yer tea, milk and sugar? The lass can try on while I go fetch the brew." He turned around at the door before leaving. "And we've got twenty other dresses ready for you for your promotion. Bejeez, never say we're not magnuminus at Amber. I feel just like Santa Claus the day right enough!"

Roslyn didn't waste time. Before Alf's kettle had boiled she had the dress on and was shedding gallons of tears again. Only this time they were caused by joy. A roll of kitchen towel on a side table sufficed as Kleenex.

"Every part of it is great, even the satin and the colour." It was good to hear. "But will you be able to adjust the width and the length ok? Even in these high heels, it's drowning me."

Certainly the gown needed taken in an inch or so. And of course it was too long, since all new wedding gowns were made to fit very tall models. All of this was standard stuff.

"Easily," I was happy to tell her. "And it isn't sales talk, honestly – but you look absolutely amazing."

She lapped up the compliment and agreed. "I love it to bits. It was all meant to be, I'm sure of it. The other dress wouldn't hold a candle to this one. Right?"

A small frown appeared right then.

"In all of this I never asked how much the dress would be, as if it wasn't important. Will it be expensive?"

"Well, since it's last season and is included in a bargain batch I'm taking from this company, I think it will be very affordable for you. Of course you'll need a headdress and veil too, to match the champagne. Amber is selling me some out of stock lines on those, too. So you could take advantage of that." I looked at her brilliant white satin slippers that she had cleverly remembered to bring. "If you dip those in a bowl of weak cold tea for half a minute they'll turn to champagne, too." I suddenly realized what I had just said.

"I mean the shoes, not the tea…" It was a dyeing trick we had employed several times.

"Great. I'm so grateful." The look of relief on her little face was cheering.

"Then all I have to pay on top is for the alterations, right?"

"Of course. Mind you, you could save on those costs too, Roslyn."

She looked intrigued and I tried not to laugh.

"Well, you don't have to use our salon. You could always ask your aunt to tackle any alterations…."

The reply was not surprising, but good natured, as she smiled broadly.

"Eh, no. No. I think I'll take a pass on that one, thank you very much!"

Princess Diana, the Queen and I – by Royal Appointment

Ballater is a delightful village in the highlands of Scotland and is an important feature on the Aberdeenshire tourist map for several reasons. Apart from the glorious setting of hills and glens, it's little shopping centre is quite unique. It boasts a profusion of small shops like the hardware shop, the newsagent, the kiltmaker all boasting large, colourful insignias above their doorways declaring: 'By Appointment to Her Majesty the Queen' or occasionally 'By Appointment to HRH The Prince of Wales'. Not a sight you see everywhere.

All of this 'lion and unicorn' decoration has happened because the Queen's highland residence, Balmoral Castle is close by. The shops have been catering to British monarchs since Queen Victoria and Prince Albert built the castle in 1856. Whilst hunting, shooting and fishing outlets are the mainstay, jewellery, fashion and gift shops are plentiful too. But the food outlets are the fascinating factor for me. The prestigious shields over the butcher or the baker shops seem to suggest the Queen might have just been out riding and after tying her horse up at the village square, popped in to pick up something for dinner. Well, who knows? The last time I visited the delightful village butcher I asked if the venison sausages were fresh and tasty. It was a foolish question, considering he had made them himself, sausage maker extraordinaire.....

"Aye, they're fresh and tasty alright! The Queen has these sausages every morning for her breakfast so if they're guid enough for her, then they're guid enough for you!"

I was put in my place and bought a pound. I don't know if the Queen enjoys haggis but I bought some of that, too.

Ballater would seem to have little to do with my company which was based near Glasgow, one hundred and twenty-five miles away as the crow flies, but as business developed, we found ourselves in the highlands frequently. Yellow Pages had us listed as 'Scotland's Complete, Unique Wedding Specialists' so off we would go regularly to deliver weddings to Fort William, Inverness, Aberdeen and even Dornoch. Dornoch is so far north that if you step outside the town you have one foot in the North Sea and are two breast strokes away from Norway.

On this occasion clients from Glasgow were being married 'away' meaning everything was happening in Braemar, another Brigadoon village on the other side of Balmoral Castle which was nestled between the two communities. Our whole team was there to supply photos, cars, video, flowers, kilts etc. Since the job was almost a three hour drive from base, some of us decided to stay over. In Scotland a three hour drive is not an excursion – it's usually considered a weekend away. The day after the wedding, Other Half and I took a hearty breakfast in our hotel, then packed our gear to travel back south, but we had a little treat in store first. We were heading to the Queen's castle to rent a couple of her ponies for a trek.

It was early summer and we were taking advantage of the Queen not being in residence then. Her highland season was usually August to October during the shooting season when NOBODY - at least no nosy tourists, got through the gates. When she is away visitors buy tickets and do tours, helping the Royal overheads. At

338

that time pony trekking was popular, but in 2012 the Queen herself decided to cease the practice, worrying about the number of overweight visitors thrusting themselves upon her poor little creatures. But this was not yet 2012 and we were not particularly overweight, so off we happily traipsed into the Royal stables with our trek leader to be assigned our ponies. The weather was fine and we were anticipating a happy jaunt around the Royal estate after the day before's busy wedding.

We were the first to arrive and had time to fuss over our two rides, a Fell and a Highland who both appreciated our chatter and fussing while the trek leader headed out to find the rest of the group. At ease in our solitude, we were focusing so much on the beautiful animals that we barely noticed the sound of footsteps approaching. I turned my head slightly, expecting another trekker to appear – and there she was. Her Majesty the Queen was standing right behind us.

"Are you taking these two out today?" she asked and nuzzled her way forward towards our ponies, joining in the stroking game. My nose was shoved out of joint completely. I had thought my sweet little Fell was taken with ME but no. When HRH touched him he turned straight to her and ignored me completely. Yes, he was in love with somebody else. And he wasn't being impressed by a diamond crown or ermine collared cape, either.

Her Majesty modestly sported an olive tweed skirt and beige well-worn cardigan over a sage silk blouse. The only salute to elegance was a single strand of pearls barely visible under her open neckline.

"Yes, Ma'am," said Other Half. Rare indeed for me, I had shifted into dumbstruck mode.

"Where are you from?" was the next question.

"We're from Coatbridge, Ma'am," he neighed in for his mute partner.

"Oh, indeed. Coatbridge…" She gave the impression she knew the place inside out. I thought of telling her which street we lived on, just in case she would know that, too. But instead, when I found my voice I became bold and asked HER a question.

"We didn't expect to meet you here today, Ma'am." Well, it was a half question and I had managed not to snort.

She didn't send me to the Tower. Instead she pleasantly explained her personal reason for being here, out of season but not out of sorts.

"I came up to see a new foal which arrived the other day. A short visit, but I had to see him. So exciting…"

You couldn't wipe the grin off her face but who would have wanted to?

With that, she indulged in another couple of pony strokes and then left, wishing us a nice day.

I held my breath for a few seconds before screaming loudly in delight. I'm sure I didn't wait long enough to vent, so unless HM was hearing impaired, she would definitely have heard. Perhaps she thought the pony hoofed me….

Unfortunately this little incident, precious as it was, gave me no right whatsoever to hammer a Royal Warranty sign over my salon door. But my meeting with Princess Diana could have resulted in me getting out my tool kit – just possibly…..

My three primary school children were on a high. They had come home with little school notes telling me that the following afternoon was to be a holiday since the most famous woman in the world, Princess Diana was to visit our town. For security reasons the advance notice to the townsfolk had been kept to a minimum. Also, the children had been given a choice of going into our town centre with their teacher and school chums or setting out with a parent or guardian. Only my eldest opted to join me so I set about preparing for the event the next morning by making up some flowers. I created a pretty posy of fresh roses and carnations for my daughter to present to the princess hoping this would entice her to stroll over to us in the crowd and give us her chat. A sort of floral carrot. I would take time off by closing the salon. It wasn't fair for me to skive off work for the afternoon and expect my employees not to, besides which the whole town would be Princess watching, not princess shopping.

It was a mile into town and a twenty minute walk for us with friends and neighbours who all decided to leave their cars parked in the driveway, rightly believing that parking in town would have been almost impossible. There were massive throngs so our group split up to find decent spaces and we two gratefully claimed a fine one right in front of Woolworths. Soon an important, glassy, classy and glossy black limo drove into the area and out came the lady herself, blonde, tall and beautiful. Her outfit was a charcoal grey cashmere collarless suit with a full skirt whilst a cream silk Peter Pan collared blouse trimmed with tiny red buttons reflected her red pump shoes. Her lady in waiting shadowed her as did the

342

security detail but she was on full show, a lovely sight to see. The Main Street was now her stage and her Coatbridge audience was overwhelmingly appreciative.

Kirsty stood holding the posy, hoping and hoping Diana would notice. She eventually did.

Suddenly she was right in front of us and smiling at the little nine year-old with the flowers.

"It's lovely. Was it made up this morning?" she asked her.

Her next move shocked me, for she took the posy and pushed it right into her gorgeous face – so firmly it seemed almost farcical. This was concerning for I knew the posy's very recent history. And it wasn't good.

On the walk into town Kirsty had insisted that SHE carry the flowers which were not covered at all, being fresh. This would have been fine but she sadly experienced slippery fingers with the poor little offering at least three times en route. It had been dropped in a deep muddy puddle, made a brief acquaintance with an old greasy slice of pizza lying on the pavement and the final indignity had been landing in a hearty mess of bird poop as we made our way under a railway bridge. It hadn't been called the Pigeon Bridge for nothing.

Kirsty told her yes, and that her mum had only just made up the formal, bridesmaid-style arrangement. Again Diana took the posy and shoved it once more into her glorious, pore-free complexion to savour the bouquet. I looked on nervously, wondering what nasty stuff was lurking in there and checking the exquisite royal skin for signs of pepperoni or bird crap which could easily have been dislodged from the folds of the fragrant petals onto the delicate visage. Definitely not a good look for this normally gorgeous icon on the evening news tv footage.

Princess Diana addressed the lady parent standing behind Kirsty and slightly glared at me, looking up from under her thick, glossy blonde fringe. I had the feeling she enjoyed talking to the children but adults seemed to be a different matter entirely. It was either that or perhaps she didn't like the smell of pizza.

"I put the flowers together this morning, Ma'am," I told her and reached out to shake her hand. Since her right hand was clutching the poor wee accident-prone posy, she offered her left hand. I felt THE RING as I shook. The large sapphire surrounded by almost neon diamonds was large and protruding and at that time a symbol of romantic, royal love. Innocent times. Her hand was cold and thin although the September weather was fine. Not Mediterranean but not Baltic, either. A nice, hot cup of tea would have done wonders for her, I was certain of that.

She commented that the flowers were just lovely yet again and went back to addressing Kirsty, smiling all the while.

"Do you like school?" was next. I believe Kirsty nodded. Not protocol, but Diana didn't care.

"Do you enjoy reading?" I had a feeling she was quite taken by my daughter. At least one of us was winning.

Then like a dream, she drifted off to another child, spreading her magical fairy princess dust and still clutching the little star-crossed bouquet. She obviously liked it for she held onto it for some time while other gifts of blooms were immediately handed over to the lady-in-waiting and put into the vehicle.

I exasperate myself on looking back at these royal meetings and regretting not having a mobile phone or camera. There were no mobiles at that time and lack of notice about the royal visit disallowed a camera for me. I usually loaded one up with film for birthdays or special occasions, generally. I'm sure others did take photos but not silly old me. Perhaps I should have run up to Boots the Chemist for a roll of film, instead of putting together the posy. But without that tough little floral offering, would Diana have come over to speak?

And another one to ponder. Would I now be eligible to place the Royal Warrant above my salon door?

I'm still not sure about that one…..

Printed in Great Britain
by Amazon

17721276R00200